# CORE BUSINESS PROGRAM

# FINANCE

By
Susan B. Rosenberg
Lawrence Dyer
D. A. Harvey
E. McLaney

**Facts On File Publications**
460 Park Avenue South
New York, N.Y. 10016

CORE BUSINESS PROGRAM
FINANCE

Susan Rosenberg, M.B.A.
Lawrence Dyer
D.A. Harvey, BSc(Econ), MSc, IPFA
E. McLaney, MA, FCA

**Copyright © 1984 by Mike Morris Productions Inc.**

Published by Facts On File, Inc.
460 Park Avenue South, New York, N.Y. 10016

First edition published in the United Kingdom in 1983 by
Mitchell Beazley London Ltd., Mill House,
87-89 Shaftesbury Avenue, London W1V 7AD, England.

**Library of Congress Cataloging in Publication Data**

Rosenberg, Susan.
Finance.

1. Finance. I. Dyer, Lawrence.    joint author.
II. Harvey, D.A.   joint author.
III. McLaney, E.   joint author.
IV. Title.
HG173.R7 1985   332   84-8063
ISBN 0-8160-0053-0

Printed and Bound in Great Britain
10 9 8 7 6 5 4 3 2 1

# Contents

# Introduction

Business organizations usually strive to achieve a variety of objectives that are frequently expressed in financial terms. These corporate objectives provide a set of criteria upon which financial decisions can be based.

In general terms, business organizations seek to achieve their objectives by **obtaining funds** from various sources and **investing** these funds in different types of assets, such as buildings, plant, machinery, vehicles, inventories of finished goods and raw materials, etc. The most fundamental decisions which management must make include choosing those forms of fund-raising and investment which will most effectively promote the achievement of the organization's objectives. The subject of finance is, broadly, the study of how best to make these decisions, and most of this book is concerned with the following aspects.

**1.** A review of the **sources and types** of funds available (Chapters 2 and 3).

**2.** A consideration of the **optimal balance** among the different types of funds, given the conflicts which exist between cost and risk (Chapters 10 and 11).

**3.** A variety of **investment decisions**, covering investment in:

  (a) fixed assets (Chapter 6);
  (b) shares and bonds (Chapter 7);
  (c) other organizations, through take-overs and mergers (Chapter 8);
  (d) current assets (Chapter 9).

It is important to recognize that the various types of funds raised each have their own **cost**, and each carries certain **risks**. For example, any form of debt must be paid or the firm will be considered in default and bankruptcy may result, whereas equity funding may expand the ownership of the firm but does not bring additional fixed costs (i.e., interest payments) with it.

Similar ideas apply to investment decisions. Those projects which the firm undertakes, whose outcomes are the most uncertain (and therefore are high risk), would probably be required to have higher *expected returns* than more certain or secure projects. A great deal of financial management is concerned with making decisions that provide a balance between **risk on the one hand, and cost or return on the other**. Attitudes towards risk vary from one person to another, and it is the responsibility of the financial manager to seek that balance which will most satisfy those parties with an interest in the organization.

In making these kinds of decisions, financial management need to understand the **environment** within which they operate. They will then be able to weigh the risks and likely returns of proposed courses of action.

This book, therefore, also includes the following aspects.

**1.** A brief review of the role of **financial markets** (Chapter 3).

**2.** An examination of the traditional methods of **financial analysis** (Chapter 4).

**3.** A general indication of how the **US taxation system** operates, and its significance in both funding and invest-ment decisions (Chapter 5).

In writing this book, we were faced with something of a dilemma since "Finance" can be taught to different types of student in a variety of ways, ranging from a simple descriptive approach, through a purely practical rendition, to an extremely theoretical treatment of the subject. The size and nature of this book preclude the latter approach. However, both the descriptive and practical approaches can be dangerously misleading, with solutions being offered without the development of a clear rationale for a particular proposal. A considerable amount of benefit has been derived from theoretical work conducted in the area of finance, and an understanding of the main **theories of finance** is considered to be essential for all but the most casual student. We have thus incorporated references to, and explanations of, the main theories of finance – albeit briefly – and have attempted to identify the basic assumptions and restrictions of these theories. This approach should make the book useful for a wide variety of courses, ranging from broadly based practical courses in finance to the more theoretical courses associated with most degrees in Business Studies.

# Chapter 1

# The Importance of Finance

## DECISION MAKING

Finance is an important aspect of most business decisions. Its significance varies from decision to decision, and a clear understanding of the way in which decisions are made is essential if the role of finance is to be seen in its true perspective.

### The decision making process

In general terms, decision making is likely to include the following stages, although some stages may be more implicit than explicit.

**1.** Determining the **objectives or goals** of the organization or individual making the decision.

**2.** Identifying any **constraints or limits on the decision maker's freedom of action**.

**3.** Identifying the various **possible courses of action** which might achieve the set objectives, subject, of course, to any of the constraints referred to above.

**4. Evaluating** the best possible course of action to be undertaken.

**5.** Ensuring by **effective control** that the planned course of action is carried out.

**6. Modifying** the course of action in the light of information newly available – frequently obtained by comparing actual results with planned action.

**7.** Ensuring the **provision of adequate data** for making further decisions.

### Business objectives

Financial decisions, like any other kind of decisions, can only be made sensibly if clear objectives are established and then used as a criterion on which to base the decision. Many suggestions have been put forward in an attempt to identify the **objectives of the typical business organization**. The most prevalent include the following:

**1. Maximizing shareholder** (or **owner**) wealth, which is similar to maximizing profit.

**2. Satisficing**, or the achievement of a satisfactory level of profits. Such a goal allows additional objectives to be achieved more easily.

**3. Survival** (though survival with no prospects of further profits may not be desirable).

**4. Sales maximization**.

**5.** The achievement of a **specified market share**.

**6. Growth** at various levels, which is a variation on the market share objective.

**7.** The **maximization of profit**.

**8. Stability**, which is sometimes seen as an end in itself.

It should also be borne in mind that while organizations may formally specify certain goals or objectives, *individuals* actually implement policy, and they often have their own career goals or aspirations. The separation of ownership and control, a result of the growth of corporations, has tended to make individual goals assume an increasing importance and a number of interesting **behavioral theories** concerning firm objectives and **managerial goals/ incentives** have been put forward (see *Organization Theory* in this series).

Certain inconsistencies and conflicts exist between the objectives cited above, though theoretically it is assumed that firms aim to maximize shareholder wealth. Nevertheless, the importance of finance is apparent in almost all cases. In practice, where goals are explicitly specified by top management, **financial goals usually appear as the single most important set of goals**. These goals are expressed in terms of required profit levels, earnings per share, required rates of return on investment, etc.

In making financial decisions, it is important to set out clear objectives. In most of the succeeding chapters, where theoretically-correct decisions are being sought, the basic objective is assumed to be the **maximization** of shareholders' or **owners' wealth**. If actual objectives differ, certain adaptations to the theoretical results may need to be made.

Maximization of shareholders' or owners' wealth recognizes that profits *per se* will not be an objective of shareholders if those profits are earned at the expense of a reduction in existing shareholders' wealth. For example, any action which would lead to a reduction in **earnings per share** would also reduce shareholder wealth and would not be consistent with this goal of the firm. It is not, therefore, likely to be the kind of decision taken by owners, who will probably be more interested in at least maintaining their own wealth. Furthermore, the search for high profits usually involves high levels of risk, with associated problems, and may, in extreme cases, cause the organization to collapse.

## Constraints on activity

In making decisions, it is usual to find that a number of constraints exist with regard to an organization's freedom of action. These include such factors as **legal** restrictions, **social** or political pressures and financial limitations. **Financial constraints** can take a variety of forms. Limitations on an organization's activity can arise simply because **inadequate financial resources** are available at a particular time to carry out all possible plans. Thus, a large part of the financial manager's job is concerned with ensuring that such constraints are kept to a minimum by making sure that funds are available as and when required. Certain constraints may be self-imposed, frequently to **reduce** risk, for example by insisting that certain minimum financial criteria are met with regard to all decisions (for instance, a specified minimum cash balance to be held at all times). Other constraints may be imposed by an **external source of funds** (i.e., banks) to give them better assurance that firms will be able to meet their obligations to them.

**Identifying and evaluating alternative courses of action.** Once the overall objectives of the organization have been identified, along with any constraints on freedom of action, management must decide on how best to achieve its objectives. The various strategies and courses of action open to management must be identified, and estimates made for each alternative, so that the best can be selected. **Financial estimates** form an extremely important part of this process, as do a variety of **financial models** which have been developed in order to assist in the making of particular decisions. The various decisions made then need to be coordinated to ensure that overall goals are achievable and to ensure the smooth implementation of plans. Detailed **financial plans** are an essential element in the coordination process.

In evaluating alternative courses of action, different levels of risk are likely to be associated with the different courses of action. This factor must be taken into consideration during the evaluation process, with the best **trade-off between risk and return** being sought.

## The exercise of control

When plans have been made, management clearly will wish to ensure that subsequent actions correspond with these plans, and some form of control system will need to be devised. **Financial control systems** provide the most comprehensive set of controls for most organizations. These systems provide managers with timely feedback on how well the firm is achieving its goals (i.e., are sales as expected?). Analysis of this information may alert managers to potential opportunities or trouble spots.

## FUNCTIONS OF THE FINANCIAL MANAGER

This description of the way in which decisions are made can

be used to determine the functions of finance, or those functions commonly carried out by a financial director or manager. However, **considerable overlap exists between the role of the financial manager and the accountant, and this needs to be recognized**.

The **accountant** is usually concerned with detailed record-keeping, and with the implementation of the budgetary control system. He is also likely to be involved in aspects of financial planning and short-term decision making, based upon management accounts. Given the nature of this book, it is clearly impossible to cover the roles of both the accountant and the financial manager in detail, and the emphasis here is on the latter. Those areas which are more commonly covered by the accountant are dealt with in *Management Accounting* in this series.

The **Financial Manager**, on the other hand, is concerned with the following aspects:

**1. Identifying** the present strengths and weaknesses of an organization – and the scope for improvements – by conducting a detailed **financial analysis**. A comparison with other organizations or earlier time-periods can be particularly useful.

**2. Planning** the **financial strategy** of the business. This involves a detailed consideration of the major financial factors of importance to the survival and/or development of the organization. It is likely to include such items as methods and levels of fund raising, profitability, the financing of expansion, etc.

**3.** The **financial appraisal** of the various possible courses of action. This includes such things as a detailed analysis of different capital projects, possible take-overs and mergers, or alternative methods of funding and their effects on the liquidity of the organization, etc. In the course of such an analysis the most efficient ways of operating should be identified.

**4.** Arranging for the **provision of funds**, when required, in the form needed, in the most economical way. This calls for a clear understanding of the types and costs of different sources of finance, and the risks associated with each.

**5.** Giving advice on the **capital structure** of an organization, after taking into account the advantages and costs of different types of funds, expectations of future costs, and future plans.

**6.** Deciding whether the firm should pay dividends or not, and if so, what proportion of earnings they should constitute. If a firm has highly profitable projects, then it should retain most or all of its earnings and stockholders will receive their return in the form of **stock price appreciation**. If the firm does not have many profitable projects, investors may prefer to receive most of their returns in the form of dividends, which they may use for their own investment purposes. A trade-off between **dividends** and **retentions** will be necessary, taking into account both the needs of the business and the wishes of its owners.

**7.** Ensuring that **assets are controlled** and used in an efficient manner. This relates to both **fixed assets** and **working capital**. Large amounts of funds are frequently tied up in **inventory, accounts receivable** (debts to the firm), and cash. In a sense, such assets are non-productive and should be kept to a minimum. However, there are risks in keeping inventory and cash at low levels in terms of lost sales and an inability to pay debts as they become due. Similarly, a low level of debtors implies a very stringent policy with regard to credit allowed to customers, and this in turn may lead to lost sales and therefore reduced profits. The management of working capital involves the same kind of trade-off between risk and return as described elsewhere.

**8.** Implicit in a number of the above points is the topic commonly referred to as **cash management**. The achievement of adequate profits may well be seen as an objective. However, survival in business dictates that funds are managed in such a way that cash (or access to cash) is always available when needed, even if the result is a reduction in profits. This requires the preparation of detailed **cash budgets** and/or **pro forma** (projected) **cash flow** statements, so that possible problems can be foreseen and avoided. Such problems may involve either a shortage of cash or an excess of cash, and financial managers must find ways of raising more funds as needed, or investing excess funds for an appropriate length of time or suggesting modifications to plans to achieve a more desirable cash flow pattern.

In carrying out these functions, financial managers are likely to draw on a number of other disciplines, notably financial and management accounting, economics, mathematics, statistics and law. They also need a sound understanding of the **financial markets** and the **tax environment** within which the organization operates.

The remainder of this book considers in more detail the most important of the above functions. However, it is worth emphasizing once again the importance of developing a proper system of **overall planning**. Decisions made with regard to particular parts of an organization must be in context, and plans must fit together into a coherent whole. Hence, decisions about capital investment usually need to be linked to decisions about financing; methods of fund raising need to be linked to decisions on capital structure; capital structure and dividend policy are intertwined; and so on. Only in a very few cases will decisions stand on their own. The financial manager, as a member of the top management team of an organization, must take an overall view, in order to make those decisions which best achieve the objectives of the organization.

# Chapter 2

# Sources of Financing – Types

Raising funds costs money, and the market for funds follows traditional economic rules relating to supply and demand. A **high demand** for funds results in a **high price**, through lower required returns. **Low demand** is associated with **higher required returns** in order to attract investors. Indeed, the market for funds is extremely efficient and responds quickly to a variety of **general factors**

1. **Government policy**, particularly
   (a) the level of **US Treasury borrowing**
   (b) Changes in the **Federal Reserve's monetary policy**
2. Changes in the level of **industrial investment**
3. Changes in the level of **bank credit**
4. Changes in the level of **savings**
5. Changes in overall **company profitability**
6. Inflows/outflows of **funds from overseas**

In addition, there are other **factors specific to a particular industry or a particular organization**, as follows:

1. The **type of industry**.
2. Changes in the **future prospects** of the industry or organization, particularly where high growth is expected.
3. The degree of **confidence in management**, possibly reinforced by some financial stake in the organization by management.
4. The **size and security** of the organization, e.g., small companies usually have to pay more for their funds because of the higher risks perceived by the providers of funds.
5. Changes in the existing **capital structure**.

The types of funds used should be chosen to best match the term of the need for funds and provide an overall balance between risk and associated costs.

## TYPES OF FUNDS

**Short term – up to one year**
1. **Trade credit**
2. Short-term **bank loans**
3. **Commercial Paper**
4. **Factoring**

**Intermediate term**
1. **Bank term-loans**
2. **Lease financing** for using/buying physical assets

**Long term**
1. **Equity/Capital** is the amount contributed by the owners of a business and is often supplemented by retaining some portion of profits.
2. **Fixed Income Securities** which include bonds, mortgages, and debentures.

Typical **reasons for requiring funds** include the following:

**1. Permanent capital needs**, for purposes of expansion.
**2. Acquisition of fixed assets**, usually to last several years. Assets such as land and buildings may require permanent capital, but in any case they involve a long-term commitment to funds. Similarly, plant and equipment generally require long-term funds.
**3. Provision of working capital.** There are two types – working capital needs that relate to several years ahead, and needs of a short-term or seasonal nature.
**4. Refinancing.** This is the provision of further funds to pay off an existing debt.

## TRADE CREDIT

Generally, a firm buys its supplies and materials on **credit** from other firms, recording the debt as an **accounts payable**. It is the largest form of short-term credit and arises out of ordinary business transactions. It must be managed carefully as it is a use of funds by which firms finance sales to customers. Therefore, a firm should make the most use of trade credit as a source of funds and, at the same time, minimize the extent to which its own funds are tied up in customer debts (accounts receivable).

## SHORT-TERM BANK LOANS AND BANK TERM-LOANS

Commercial bank loans appear on the balance sheet as **notes payable** and are the second important source of short-term financing. These loans are similar to personal loans in that a **promissory note** is signed and the loan is repaid either in a lump sum at maturity or in installments during the life of the loan.

Another form the loan may take is as a **line of credit**. The bank allows a firm to overdraw its checking account up to an agreed amount and charges interest on the amount of the overdraft.

Term-loans are loans with maturity of one year or more and are usually amortizing.

**Raising loans** – the mechanics of borrowing
In considering requests for loans, **bank lending officers** are likely to ask a **number of questions** to which the Financial Manager should be able to provide satisfactory answers. These questions might include the following:

**1. Why** is the loan needed?
**2. How much** is needed?
**3. How** and **when** is it to be repaid?
**4. Is the business strong** enough to keep going even if the plans are not completely successful?
**5.** What **security** is offered?
**6.** Are the **assets** of the organization marketable? Is their value steady or rising?

**7.** Are **earnings** stable?
**8. What cover** exists for the loan, i.e., what is the relationship between the total market value of an organization's assets and its outside debts?

## COMMERCIAL PAPER

Commercial Paper consists of promissory notes of **large** firms sold primarily to other businesses, pension funds, insurance companies and banks. Maturities vary from two to six months. An advantage of this type of financing is that the interest rate it carries is often below that on prime business loans.

## FACTORING

Factoring is a **financial and administrative service** designed to relieve management of certain routine financial matters, thus freeing management time for other activities. Factoring tends to be aimed at small- to medium-sized organizations.

Basically, a factor offers three types of service, although there is usually no pressure to accept all three.

**1. An organizational service.** The factor effectively takes over the accounts section of the client – sending out invoices, making collections from debtors and keeping the debtor's ledger up to date.

**2. An insurance service.** Some protection for bad debts is provided.

**3. A cash-flow service.** The client receives up to about 80% of the value of a sales invoice as soon as it is sent to the customer. The remaining money is then passed on to the client after the factor has gathered it in.

## LEASE-FINANCING

Many firms are interested in leasing buildings and equipment rather than owning them, particularly when there are no **tax advantages** to ownership. Other firms may use amortizing leases to purchase the plant or equipment.

Leasing works in the following way: The lessee company selects the asset. The leasing company purchases it. The lessee uses the asset and pays a rent. Regular payments are made, usually monthly, and are normally of a fixed amount. The financial commitment is thus easily understood and this aspect of leasing has distinct attractions for businessmen.

There are few **restrictions** on leasing, but in general terms, the asset to be leased should be clearly and easily identifiable and have a lifetime at least as long as the period of the lease agreement.

**Service leases** are usually used for equipment which the lessor maintains for the user. These leases are used for high technology equipment, e.g., computers, where rapid obsolescence is the norm because they can be cancelled if the equipment becomes out-dated.

When the lease payments contribute to the purchase of the asset, an **investment tax credit** is allowed up to the amount of the firm's taxes. Otherwise, the main advantage to leasing is that the payments are **tax-deductible** expenses.

## EQUITY/CAPITAL

In simple terms, equity/capital is the contribution to the funds of a business by the owner(s).

In a **one-man company**, the owner provides the funds, usually makes the decisions, and is entitled to the profits which result. He also takes the risks and, in the event of the failure of the business, stands to lose all his capital/equity, **and** is personally liable for any outstanding debts.

In a **partnership**, a number of individuals operate together, each contributing an agreed amount of capital in return for an agreed share of the profits. There are two types of partners; **general partners** have voting rights, and thus control the partnership, but are personally liable for the firm's debts. **Limited partners** do not have voting rights, but are only liable for their initial investment in the firm. In a partnership, the firm is not subject to income taxes; the partners are taxed on a personal basis for their share of the firm's net income.

In the case of an **incorporated company**, i.e., a **corporation**, one or many individuals provide part of the agreed capital. In exchange, investors are given share certificates of the company. A share of the company gives its owner one vote in determining how the company should be run, and one share of the company's profits. The shareholders are **not personally liable** for the firm's debts; once they have paid in the agreed value of their share of the capital they cannot be asked to provide further funds. If the firm goes bankrupt, shareholders run the risk of losing money to the extent of their investment, but their **liability is limited** to this amount.

The **incorporated company** provides the opportunity for a large number of people to become owners, and so paves the way for much larger organizations. With large corporations that have millions of shares, it is impossible for all the shareholders to participate in the running of the firm, so shareholders choose a board of directors to run the company for them.

A further advantage of the corporation is that individual shareholders are able to sell their shares without affecting the legal identity of the company. This permits shareholders a greater degree of flexibility than is possible for the sole trader or partnership. In practice, the degree of flexibility for the transfer of ownership depends on whether the company is:

1. **Private** or **public**
2. **Listed** or **Unlisted**

A **public corporation** has no limit on the number of shareholders it can have and is free to offer new shares to the public. There are no restrictions on the transfer of shares and a market exists for second-hand shares. Public companies tend to be large. A market for these "second-hand" shares can be found in the various **stock exchanges**, e.g., The New York Stock Exchange, that exist. These exchanges provide a **market** for those securities which are "quoted" on them. Except for the Over-The-Counter-Market, which is an informal medium for trading shares, certain fairly rigorous conditions need to be satisfied before a firm is "listed" on an exchange. The shares of listed companies thus have a greater marketability than those of unlisted companies.

Shareholders obtain a **return on their investment** in the form of **dividends** (either cash or stock) and/or **increases in the value of their shares**. It should be noted that the **par value** of a share bears no relation to the **market value**. Typically, the **market value** of a share far exceeds the par value.

## TYPES OF SHARES

Shares fall into the two major categories given below.

1. **Common** shares
2. **Preferred** shares

Common shares are the main risk-bearing security of a business. Profits accrue to common shareholders only **after** all other claims have been met. If profits are high, dividends and/or increases in the value of the shares will also be high. If profits are low, or losses are made, dividends will be low or non-existent. In the event of liquidation of a firm, the common shareholder's claim on the business will be paid only after all other claims have been paid. However, as the risk-bearing security, each common share carries with it one vote at company meetings. Hence, it is the common shareholders who ultimately control the company through their ability to choose and change the board of directors.

**Preferred shares** are shares which carry with them a prior claim to profits. Dividends, which are payments to shareholders, must be paid to preferred shareholders first, if they are paid at all, and then to common shareholders. In the event of a liquidation, preferred shareholders have a prior claim on the firm's assets over common shareholders, although all outside lenders/creditors, etc., have priority over preferred shareholders.

A variety of ways exist in which equity capital can be raised. Most of the alternatives are dealt with in the following chapter.

**Stock dividends** are dividends in the form of new shares that are paid to existing shareholders in proportion to their holdings.

**Rights Issues.** A rights issue is an offer to existing shareholders of a **right** to acquire further shares in proportion to the shareholder's existing shareholdings. These are usually offered at a price which is below the current market price. Since rights can be sold, shareholders who do not wish to take up the offer are allowed to sell their rights to others who would use it. This ensures that most rights issues are successful.

The advantages to a company of a rights issue are given below.

**1. Cheapness.** Since issues are available only to existing shareholders, no advertising costs, audits, etc., are incurred and administrative costs are low.

**2. Control** over a company is maintained by the existing shareholders, since rights are issued in proportion to existing holdings.

**Example.** A company has 100,000 shares, with a market value of $2.50 each, makes a rights issue on a 1-for-5 basis at a price of $1.50 per share. The market value of the company before the rights offering is $250,000. An issue on a 1-for-5 basis means that for each holding of five shares, shareholders will be given the right to acquire one new share at a price of $1.50. If the rights are taken up, 20,000 new shares would be issued at a price of $1.50 each, resulting in a $30,000 inflow into the company. Other things being equal, the company's market value will increase to $280,000. Since the number of shares issued will now be 120,000, the **market price per share** is likely to fall to approximately $280,000/120,000, which equals $2.33 per share.

In making a comparison between the two situations outlined above – before and after the rights issue was raised – for a holding of five shares we obtain the following:

**Before** rights offering
5 shares at $2.50 = $12.50
Exercise of the right
$1.50 payment for the sixth share, must be added to this to give:
Total investment = $14

**After** rights are exercised
6 shares at $2.33 each = $14

Rights would be sold at a price approximating the difference between the offer price of $1.50 and the estimated price eacafter issue of $2.33. Hence, a shareholder who sold his rights would be faced with the following situation.

**Before** rights offering
5 shares at $2.50 each = $12.50

**After**
5 shares at $2.33 each = $11.67
Plus proceeds of rights issue at 83¢ = $12.50

In practice, it is unlikely that prices will change with the precision implied above, but the principles remain. In fact, rights issues are frequently associated with expansion or an improvement in prospects, so the value of shares after the rights issue may well be **higher** than would have been suggested using the above approach.

A **stock split** is an action to increase the number of shares outstanding by a multiple of some number. For example, a 3-for-1 stock split would give every shareholder three shares for every share that he/she previously held. There is no change in the balance sheet of the company; it is just divided into smaller pieces. It is often held that stock splits occur when the market price per share is very high and out of the reach of the ordinary investor. Further, the market may interpret a stock split as a signal that the managers of the company expect its share price to rise rapidly.

### Retained earnings
Profits are probably the most important source of funds. Some profits are distributed to owners in the form of dividends, while some are retained for investment inside the firm in an account called **retained earnings**.

## FIXED-INCOME SECURITIES
**Long-term promissory notes** which have regularly scheduled interest payments are known as fixed-income securities because the lenders receive those payments according to a schedule. Whether a firm has profits or losses, it must pay the interest or **coupon payment**, as it is known, or be deemed in **default**, in which case all of its assets are subject to claims by the bondholders.

Companies can issue bonds with different types of claims:

**1.** A **bond** is a promissory note which is sometimes secured by particular assets of the firm. If the firm goes bankrupt, the bond is paid off through the sale of those assets. If the secured assets are insufficient, the bondholder has a claim on all of the firm's unsecured assets.

**2.** A **debenture** is an unsecured bond which makes it more costly to issue. The firm has to pay a higher borrowing rate on it because it is paid off only before equity claims if the firm defaults.

**3.** A **mortgage bond** is a bond which is secured by a claim to property and/or buildings. These are typically the most secure assets of the firm.

## INFLUENCES ON THE CHOICE OF FINANCING

In practice, one will find a variety of sources of funding being used. As outlined in this chapter, different types of financing have different advantages and disadvantages and a balanced set of liabilities offers maximum benefit. Once the length of time the funds are needed is determined, the major trade-off is between costs and risks. For example, long-term debt usually costs more than short-term debt, but it also reduces the likelihood that a short-term liquidity crisis will occur. Higher levels of equity, which appear to be cheaper when interest rates are high, may result in dilution of the claims of existing owners.

The other important considerations are:

**1.** The interest payments on debt are **tax-deductible expenses**, making it cheaper than equity if the firm pays dividends. On the other hand, cash dividends are paid out of net income after taxes, so there is no threat to the solvency of the firm.

**2.** The **use of debt** has distinct advantages due to the fact that increases in the level of debt involves increases in the firm's **fixed costs**, which in turn increases the likelihood of insolvency (see Chapter 11).

In sum: It must be noted that the cost of funds will depend on the length of time the funds are invested and the risk of the investment.

Investors have different preferences for the length of the investment period. This results in different costs of obtaining funds for different periods. Typically the cost of funds for a short-term investment (e.g. one year) is less than the cost of funds for a long-term investment (e.g. thirty years). While the costs of borrowing short term are less, the risks to the borrower are greater. He is exposed to changes in the interest rate and the potential of a short-term liquidity crisis.

The risk of the firm is packaged in the securities that it uses to obtain funds. The cost of obtaining funds with different securities reflects the risk of the security and the maturity of the security.

Equity is riskier than debt and therefore equity must offer a higher return to investors than debt. But as a firm issues more debt, the cost of the debt increases. This is because the debt holders bear more risk as the amount of debt increases.

The factors that affect the firm's decision on issuing securities are quite complex. Most large firms find that they

obtain the most favorable terms on funds by using a variety
of sources. Chapters 10 and 11 discuss the factors that affect
the firm's capital structure.

# Chapter 3

# Sources of Funds – Institutional

Firms deal with a variety of organizations that either provide funds or assist the firms in obtaining those funds. The institutions most commonly involved in such activities are:

1. **Commercial Banks**
2. **Investment Banks**
3. **Other Institutional Backers**
   (a) **Venture Capital Firms**
   (b) **Pension Funds**
   (c) **Insurance Companies**
4. **Small Business Administration**
5. **The New Issue Market**

In addition to the above, the role and operation of the **New York Stock Exchange** and the **Over-The-Counter Market** will be examined, in view of the importance of these markets for second-hand securities – secondary markets – in fund-raising activities.

## COMMERCIAL BANKS

Commercial banks play an extremely important role in providing certain types of financing. For relatively small firms, commercial banks are often the only source of outside financing. The **principal types of loans** that are available are as follows:

**1.** The **overdraft** is used for short-term liquidity crunches, seasonal problems and similar temporary needs.

**2. Commercial loans** are obtained by industrial and commercial customers of the bank. The term of the loan can vary from about ninety days to seven years. Banks often require that borrowers keep from 10 to 20% of the loan in an account at the bank, or be charged a higher loan rate. The loan may be **secured** by an asset of the firm, in which case a more favorable loan rate is charged.

Commercial loans may be obtained for the following purposes:
**(a)** Acquisition of new premises;
**(b)** Extensions of, or improvements to, existing buildings;
**(c)** Acquisitions of, and mergers with, other businesses.

**3. Revolving line-of-credit** is an agreement between the bank and its customer whereby the bank promises to extend a line-of-credit during the term of the agreement. The customer can turn it into a term loan simply by borrowing when the need arises.

In **applying for a bank loan** the following factors need to be considered.

**1.** The **reason** for wanting financial assistance must be identified, and then the appropriate **type** of loan applied for.

**2. Detailed estimates**, clearly setting out the estimated needs, should be made to support the case for the loan. These estimates enable the bank to see that the method and timing of repayments have been carefully thought through. The **cash-flow effects** of any proposition must be clearly demonstrated.

**3.** Plans are not always achieved in their entirety and questions are likely to be raised by the bank about **contingency plans** in the event that difficulties arise.

**4.** It must be remembered that banks are not in business to put their capital at unnecessary risk and they usually require **adequate security** for loans. In general, it may be said that banks are more concerned with the safety of their loans rather than the level of profits that might accrue from investment by the borrower.

## INVESTMENT BANKS

Investment banks are not a direct source of funds. While commercial banks lend their own funds, investment banks serve as intermediaries between firms and investors. They provide advice to firms and place the firms' securities with investors, who provide the external source of funds.

The following is a list of the principal activities in which investment banks are engaged.

**1. Underwriting** is the process of both assisting in the issuance of new securities and insuring a new issue against adverse price movements during the time of distribution.

For example, suppose a firm needs $10 million; it picks an underwriter and, in conference, decides to issue bonds on a certain date at a chosen coupon rate. On that date, the underwriter gives the firm a check for $10 million and, in return, receives 10,000 bonds in $1,000 denominations. From the time the underwriter pays the firm $1 million (less commission) until all of the bonds are sold, which may take several days, the underwriter bears all the risk of fluctuations in the market price of the bonds.

**2. Distribution.** The next function of investment banks is to market securities. Investment banks employ **stockbrokers** and **bondbrokers** to sell securities, for which they are paid a commission. While the issues can be new, they are often outstanding securities which are traded in existing markets, i.e., the New York Stock Exchange, the American Stock Exchange.

**3. Advisors.** Since the primary functions of investment banks are to create and market securities, they are experts in tailoring the characteristics of the securities to match the demands of investors. If matched correctly, a new issue should be sold the day it is put on the market. Hence, an investment banker's reputation hinges on the degree of success attained in marketing a security. Often, investment bankers will sit on the board of directors of the firms they have counseled in order to increase the firm's chances of success. In this way, decisions are made which simultaneously satisfy both the firm's needs and investor demands.

## OTHER INSTITUTIONAL BACKERS

### Venture capital firms
**Venture capital firms** (which are sometimes owned by investment banks) provide **investment capital** for the creation and/or expansion of new companies. These companies are generally young and their managements inexperienced, so there is a great deal of **risk involved in investing** in them. Venture capital firms will often require a share in the company's equity in exchange for funds, with the expectation of taking the company **public**, i.e., selling shares in one of the organized markets in the near future to reclaim their funds.

### Pension funds
Many employees (and employers) pay contributions into pension funds, with a view to ensuring that adequate pensions will be available for their retirement. Such funds must be invested to enable the pension fund to accumulate and grow, thus ensuring that adequate funds are always available when required. Vast sums are now involved. For example, pension funds are the largest institutional owners of stock in the United States, and the third largest owners of bonds.

### Insurance companies
Insurance companies, like pension funds, are large institutional investors in stocks, bonds and real estate. In addition, they use their funds as investment capital in making mortgage loans on commercial and industrial properties to small firms, although arranging such loans requires extra effort and expense.

## SMALL BUSINESS ADMINISTRATION

The Small Business Administration (SBA) was created by Congress in 1953 to help small firms as follows:

**1.** To aid in the **acquisition of government contracts**.
**2.** To **offer loans to small firms** unable to obtain private financing at reasonable terms.
**3.** To **provide technical and managerial guidance** for small firms.

**4.** To **administer government funds** specifically allocated for businesses that have been damaged and are in need of rehabilitation.

To be eligible for assistance by the SBA, firms must meet various size standards. To name one definition: a firm which is independently owned and operated, not dominant in its field, without a public market for its common stock, total assets less than $5 million, net worth under $2.5 million, and average annual net income after taxes of $250,000 during the preceding two years.

## THE NEW ISSUE MARKET

One method for a firm to raise funds is to offer its stock to the public. The three ways to do this are to apply for a **listing** on an exchange such as **The New York Stock Exchange**, or sell it to brokers on the informal **Over-The-Counter Market**, or to do a private placement, which means selling the entire issue to a small number of institutional investors via an investment bank. Following is a discussion of the process by which new issues come up for sale.

Securities-trading in the United States is regulated by the **Securities and Exchange Commission** – the **SEC**. Created by the Securities Act of 1933, its aim is to ensure **full disclosure** of relevant information and a **record of representations**. After a firm and its investment banker have reached an agreement on all aspects of the issue (except its price), the firm has been audited by a public accounting firm, and the legal aspects examined by a law firm, **registration statements** for the SEC are then prepared to explain the firm's financial condition along with its intended use of funds to be garnered by the sale of the issues.

The SEC requires a **20-day waiting period**, during which time its staff examines the registration statements to determine whether there are any misrepresentations or deletions. During this time, the securities are barred from sale, although preliminary **prospectuses** may be drawn up. A **prospectus** contains a considerable amount of detail, the most important aspects of which are outlined below.

**1.** Details of the nature of the business.
**2.** An analysis of the main trading items during the past five years.
**3.** A statement of the financial and business prospects of the firm.
**4.** An auditor's report on profitability during the past years.

The price the investment banker/underwriter actually pays for the issues is not generally decided until the end of the 20-day waiting period. There is no universal rule for determining the price. However, it is often agreed to be several percentage points below the close of the company's stock, if it is already publicly traded, on the last day of the

registration period. Otherwise, the investment banker com-
pares the firm and its prospects to other firms in the same
industry and chooses a price which is relative to the value of
the shares of the other firms.

The investment banker working with the firm will not
generally handle the purchase and distribution of the
securities alone. Other investment bankers will be invited to
form an **underwriting syndicate** which, as a whole, will
bear the risk that the price of the securities will decline
between the time they are bought from the firm and sold to
investors.

In the final analysis it is the **investors** who determine
whether or not the issue is a success, and they will usually
consider the following aspects.

**1.** The quality of management.
**2.** The purpose of the issue.
**3.** The financial forecasts, particularly when related to past
accounts and profit trends.
**4.** The capital structure.
**5.** The likely security price when dealings commence.

## Role and operation of formal exchanges

If the public is to be persuaded to make a long-term investment in an organization it will require the following.

**1.** Confidence that the investment is likely to be a profitable one.
**2.** Ability to turn investments back into cash as and when
the investor requires.

Given these requirements for the public to invest, markets
in second-hand securities (stocks and bonds) have evolved.
These markets bring together those who want to sell their
securities with those who wish to buy them. Thus, investors
are able to **liquidate** their investment in a particular firm
without such action having any direct effect on that firm.
There are many stock exchanges in the US, The New York
Stock Exchange being the largest. The next section will
discuss the NYSE; however, it should be noted that much of
what is said about the NYSE is true of stock exchanges
throughout the world.

For a stock exchange to establish credibility with the investing public, it is essential that deals are conducted in an
orderly fashion, with all investors, regardless of size of holdings, treated similarly. It is also true that if all investors have
access to the same information, then securities will be priced
in a rational way, reflecting what is known about a firm and
believed to be its future prospects.

An assessment of **fairness** in dealing and "efficiency" in
pricing will be made after a discussion of the
Over-The-Counter Market which will follow the next
section.

**Operation of The New York Stock Exchange (NYSE)**.
The NYSE is housed in a building in New York City in an
area known as **"Wall Street"**. Trading on the floor is
restricted to members of the exchange and is not open to the
general public, except as spectators in a visitors' gallery. The
privilege of membership is termed a **seat** and carries with it
the right to engage in trading. The number of seats on the
Exchange is roughly 1,300, each of which is considered an
asset whose value depends on the volume of trading and the
level of profits at any point in time.

The members of the exchange can be classified into groups
according to the function they perform. A trader may play
different or a combination of roles at various times. Following is a list of the general types of traders on the floor of the
Exchange:

**1. Commission brokers** act as agents for brokerage firms
and execute the orders of the firms' customers, who pay the
brokers a commission for that service.

**2. Floor brokers** act to aid commission brokers, who are
often unable to handle the large volume of trades that they
receive. They generally charge a flat-fee for their assistance
and do not have the overhead costs that firms employing
commission brokers have.

**3. Registered floor brokers** are traders who buy and sell
for their own accounts, although they also may act as commission brokers or floor brokers.

**4. Specialists** are, as the name implies, traders who trade
in a limited number of securities. Since the trading floor is
large and brokers cannot be everywhere at once, specialists
stay at posts where the auction is held for the particular
securities they deal in. Often investors will give, buy or sell
orders to their brokers at specific prices. If the price of the
security is different from the price specified when the order
reaches the trading floor, the order is not executed. It then
becomes the specialist's responsibility to record the
unexecuted order in his book and to ensure that it is
executed if the market price of the security reaches the
stipulated level.

Stock exchanges require firms to meet certain requirements
before they are **listed**. While the requirements depend on
the particular exchange, they relate to the size of the firm,
earnings record, number of years in business, number of
shares outstanding and their market value. In this, the
NYSE has the strictest standards.

**The Over-The-Counter Markets**
In contrast to the formal NYSE, the **Over-The-Counter
Markets** are broadly defined as all security transactions that
do not take place on an organized exchange. Instead, it is a
network of brokers throughout the country who execute
their orders electronically. Since many stocks to not trade

actively (few buy and sell orders come in), brokers maintain an inventory of them – buying when investors sell and vice versa. While a firm does not have to meet the requirements imposed by a formal exchange, approval of the SEC is necessary to have its securities traded publicly.

## "Efficiency" in security pricing

If investors are to be persuaded to invest in securities traded publicly, they will require these securities to be priced in a rational and efficient way. Securities are said to be "efficiently" priced when their current price reflects their "true" worth at all times. It is impossible for us to know whether or not the securities dealt with are efficiently priced or not, simply because we do not know what the "true" worth of any particular security is. A security, like any other asset, e.g. an automobile, will be viewed by different people in different ways.

Having said this, it must be remembered that the securities markets are open and competitive, and trading prices reflect the consensus view of all investors, who, by acting as either buyers or sellers of a particular security, affect its price. Efficiency could therefore be construed to imply that security prices should react quickly and logically to new information likely to affect the security's "true" worth. In fact, most research findings suggest that this does occur, and that security prices do move quickly (within a few minutes of new information becoming available) and in the direction that one would expect.

Academics describe three types of market efficiency: weak, semi-strong and strong. These three types of market efficiency specify the type of information incorporated in stock prices. There is strong empirical support for the first two types of market efficiency; the empirical support for the third type of market efficiency is mixed.

The *weak* form of market efficiency specifies that all of the information in past prices is incorporated in the current price. This argument implies that changes in prices follow a random pattern.

Investors will not outperform the market after adjustments for the risk of their investments by using information based on past prices.

The *semi-strong* form of market efficiency states that all publicly available information is incorporated in the market prices. Thus the use of any publicly available information, such as dividend or earnings increases, will not lead to superior investment performance after adjusting for risk.

The *strong* form of market efficiency specifies that all available information, both public and private, is incorporated into the current market price. The results of the empirical research in this area are mixed. The market price may not reflect all private information, but the extra return from the private information compensates the industrious investors for their research. Some of the private information is reflected in stock prices, limiting the returns to collecting information.

## Conclusions about securities markets
**1.** Fairness and equality in treatment of investors.
**2.** Rational pricing of securities at all times.

The **SEC** is vigilant in its protection of investors and adverse public criticism in this regard is extremely rare. Although price efficiency has not been proved to exist, most evidence suggests that it does.

There appears to be no real evidence that any doubts which the public may have about fairness in dealing or efficiency in pricing cause resistance by investors to taking up new issues of long-term securities.

# Chapter 4

# Financial Analysis

## GENERAL APPROACH

Most business decisions are based on estimates of future events, their associated returns and the likely risks involved. Information about past and present activities and their results are the most important source on which estimates about the future are based. Rigorous **analysis of current performance and financial position** is usually seen as a **necessary prerequisite** to most important business decisions. Information about the environment in which the firm exists (i.e., the US economy, the particular industry), etc., can be obtained from a variety of sources such as financial/economic publications, statistical services, credit agencies, etc. This section is particularly concerned with the analysis and interpretation of past accounting information.

In assessing performance, or predicting likely future events, **comparisons** will need to be made, and financial analysis frequently includes comparisons of changing economic conditions, of industries, of organizations within an industry and of figures for a particular organization over a given period of time. The use of ratios on a comparative basis can be extremely helpful and the majority of this chapter is concerned with their calculation and use.

Given that the aim of financial analysis is to help in assessing *past* performance, with a view to assisting in making decisions about the *future,* an analysis should concentrate on two areas.

**1.** It should be concerned with the identification of significant **trends and relationships**, over time, between firms and/or between industries.

**2.** It must clearly identify any **major changes** that have occurred, or are likely to occur, which would invalidate predictions based on past trends.

In practice, detailed methods of financial analysis vary considerably, but all should include detailed analysis, usually on a comparative basis, of the following:

**1.** Profit and loss statement.

**2.** Balance sheet.

**3.** Flow of funds statement.

### Profit and loss statement
An analysis of this statement has the following **aims**.

**1.** Identification of trends in income.

**2.** Assessment of the significance of different revenues or expenses with regard to overall profitability.

**3.** Isolation of factors which might indicate a change in circumstances.

The examination of the profit and loss statement would normally include the following items.

**1.** Level of sales, sales breakdowns by product and/or geographical areas, gross margins, etc., with a view to **identifying areas of growth or contraction**.

**2.** Relative proportions of different kinds of overhead expenses and their likely **future behavior**.

**3.** Amounts spent on **research and development**, and their productivity.

**4.** Depreciation and associated policies.

**5.** Non-recurring or **unusual items**.

**6.** Contributions from **overseas operations**, which are often of a rather different quality than domestic earnings.

If past information of this type is to be used to make estimates of future earnings, a number of **other considerations** will need to be borne in mind.

**1.** Economic conditions within the economy and the industry as a whole.
**2.** Research productivity and the rate of change of technology within the industry.
**3.** Current and potential competition.
**4.** The present investment in plant and machinery, and future investment needs.
**5.** Current and potential labor relations.

In considering these the analyst will usually need to look much further afield to obtain satisfactory answers..

**Balance sheet**
An examination of the balance sheet mainly focuses on **working capital** and **capital structure**, although an analysis of fixed assets and changes therein can prove useful. Consideration will need to be given to the following areas.

**1.** *Levels of working capital.* Are **inventory** and **accounts receivables** too high or too low? Are cash balances adequate?

**2.** *Levels of debt.* This is referred to as **leverage**, which has both advantages and disadvantages, depending upon the relationship between company profitability and the interest payable on debt (see Chapter 11).

**3.** Is there any debt due for repayment in the near future?

The balance sheet, by providing information (albeit imper-

fect information) on **fixed assets**, also provides something
of a guide to the capital investment of an individual organization and to its future capital investment needs.

### Flow of funds statement

The emphasis of the funds statement is on **liquidity**, which is
an essential part of financial analysis. Once again, trends
and unusual items need to be isolated. Trends will usually
relate to patterns of fixed asset acquisition, working capital
levels and dividend payments. The raising and repayment of
debt tends to be less regular, particularly where large
amounts are involved. New issues of shares, or redemption
of preferred shares, tend to be even less common. Analysis
of this type should enable very good estimates of future cash
flows to be made, since regular flows can be clearly identified and included in future estimates, while unusual items,
although also clearly identified, will not normally be repeat-
able and are, therefore, less likely to need inclusion.

## THE USE OF RATIOS IN FINANCIAL ANALYSIS

### Types of ratios

A great many questions need to be answered in a full financial analysis, and a systematic approach is therefore needed.
In practice, most analyses include the calculation of a
number of ratios which concentrate on key issues or areas
concerning an organization. The **main areas** for which
ratios are calculated are given below.

1. Profitability and asset utilization.
2. Long-term capital structure and capital intensity.
3. Liquidity and working capital.
4. Security.
5. Ordinary shares.

Detailed ratios are dealt with in the sections below. Having
said this, it must be recognized that many of the questions
posed are impossible to answer from the published accounts
alone. In practice, investment analysts tend to concentrate
on particular industries or types of business, thus building
up a specialist knowledge of the firms they analyze which
gives them a better chance of answering the appropriate
questions.

### Profitability and asset utility ratios

**Rate of return on investment** This ratio relates returns to
the amount invested. It can be calculated and interpreted in
a variety of ways, the two most usual being given below.

**1. Return on total assets**. This ratio is calculated as follows:

$$\frac{\text{Net income after taxes}}{\text{Total assets}} \times 100\%$$

Net income is taken after taxes. Non-recurring income is

usually excluded from the calculation. This ratio is one of the most useful for inter-company comparison of profitability.

**2. Return on equity**. This ratio is calculated as follows:

$$\frac{\text{Net income after taxes and preferred dividends}}{\text{Average book value per share}} \times 100$$

It provides a measure of the percentage return on the investment made by the owners, which subsequently provides a basis for comparison with alternative uses of shareholders' funds (e.g., government securities, company debentures, other shares, etc.). In turn, this is likely to reflect on future fund-raising ability.

**Return on investment** is expressed as a percentage. Generally, the higher the return the better. The rate of return on investment is dependent upon two factors – the size of the net profit margin and the efficiency of asset use.

The **net profit margin** is calculated as follows:

$$\frac{\text{Net profit after taxes}}{\text{Sales}} \times 100$$

It indicates a company's ability to generate profits from sales.

The sales to total assets is calculated as follows:

$$\frac{\text{Sales}}{\text{Average total assets}}$$

It measures a company's ability to generate sales from its assets. Pressure on, or changes in, the margin or turnover rate needs to be considered when assessing likely future profitability.

**Long-term capital structure and capital intensity ratios**
The main ratio calculated in this area is known as the debt/equity ratio. This ratio is concerned with establishing the **relationship between external and internal long-term financing**. The use of long-term debt in the capital structure has both advantages and disadvantages, and in practice the level of debt actually existing is the result of a balancing process.

One **advantage of debt** is that it provides an opportunity for greater returns to shareholders without the need to provide greater amounts of capital. Another important advantage is that the interest payments are tax-deductible, often making it cheaper to use than equity. If a company can borrow funds at a predetermined rate of interest, but use these funds in the business to obtain a greater return, all of the extra benefit accrues to the common shareholders. The more borrowed funds there are, the greater the potential returns to the common shareholders, and the greater the risks due to the increased fixed costs (interest payments), which increase the variability of the firm's earnings and the firm's chances of bankruptcy.

The leverage of the firm can be calculated in a number of ways, the two most common of which are given below.

$$\frac{\text{Long-term debt}}{\text{Long-term debt plus equity}} = \textbf{Financial leverage}$$

$$\frac{\text{Long-term debt}}{\text{Equity}} = \textbf{Debt equity ratio}$$

Care must be taken in making comparisons to ensure comparability of the ratios. Debt/equity ratios sometimes refer to total debt rather than simply long-term debt, resulting in the following type of ratio.

$$\frac{\text{Total liabilities}}{\text{Equity plus total liabilities}}$$

Also, note that the ratios typically refer to **book value**. Some ratios (e.g., debt to equity) may be calculated with either book or market values. If the results differ, market values are usually considered to give a better indication of the firm's condition.

**Capital intensity** can be measured by ratios such as:

$$\frac{\text{Fixed assets}}{\text{Total assets}}$$

This ratio indicates the proportion of total assets taken up by fixed assets. The higher the ratio, the higher the capital intensity. Manufacturing firms are likely to have rather higher ratios than trading concerns.

What is known as a **common size balance sheet** can also be useful for comparing relative asset structures and capital intensity. All items in the balance sheet are expressed as percentages of the total assets or liabilities. A comparison of the percentages for different firms, or for the same firm over time, can identify areas which need further detailed investigation. (It is perhaps worth noting that the same principle can usefully be applied to profit and loss statements, and significant changes in costs can then easily be identified.)

**Liquidity and working capital**
Liquidity and working capital assessments are made for purposes of assessing the **adequacy of liquid resources** and identifying potential problems in this area. Creditors and lenders are particularly interested in an organization's ability to service and pay off debts. Liquidity ratios provide

an indication of security. Ratios which are commonly used are described in the following sections.

## Current ratio

$$\frac{\text{Current assets}}{\text{Current liabilities}}$$

This ratio is concerned with the assessment of an organization's ability to meet its short-term obligations. Current assets must be sufficient to meet obligations, so the ratio must be high enough for safety. However, high current assets do not normally lead to high profits in themselves and so the usual trade-off between risk and return exists. For example, if **accounts receivable** are high, the current assets will be high, but the firm may have trouble obtaining the cash it needs to pay its bills.

## Quick or acid test ratio

$$\frac{\text{Current assets less inventories}}{\text{Current liabilities}}$$

This ratio is also concerned with short-term liquidity. In a sense, it is a more appropriate measure than the current ratio, since liquid assets represent the source of funds from which current liabilities will probably be met. For safety, liquid assets ought to exceed current liabilities. A ratio of 1:1, therefore, represents a theoretical minimum.

## Receivables turnover

$$\frac{\text{Sales}}{\text{Average accounts receivable}}$$

This figure measures the average number of times a year that accounts receivables change. It may also be expressed as an average **collection period**.

$$\frac{\text{Average accounts receivable}}{\text{Sales}} \times 365$$

The resulting figure measures the average number of days' credit given to debtors. Both ratios are concerned with the same thing, namely assessing the efficiency of debt collection. From an organization's viewpoint, debt collection periods should be kept as low as possible, consistent with maintaining customer goodwill. A low average debt collection period is equivalent to a high accounts receivable turnover figure.

## Inventory turnover

$$\frac{\text{Cost of goods sold}}{\text{Average inventory}}$$

This figure measures the average number of times a year that stock changes. It may also be expressed as an **average inventory holding period**.

$$\frac{\text{Average inventory}}{\text{Cost of goods sold}} \times 365$$

This figure measures the average number of days for which inventory is held.

Both ratios are concerned with measuring the efficiency of inventory utilization. The more times inventory can be turned over in a year, the more efficient an organization tends to be. Where the cost of goods sold is not known, it is quite common to substitute sales in the ratios. The resulting figures will not be as accurate, but can still be useful in isolating differences over time or between companies in the same industry.

### Creditors turnover

$$\frac{\text{Credit purchases}}{\text{Average creditors}}$$

This figure measures the number of times a year that creditors change. Alternatively, it may be expressed as a **credit period**.

$$\frac{\text{Average creditors}}{\text{Credit purchases}} \times 365$$

### Security
A number of ratios can be calculated specifically to provide an assessment of the security available for creditors, lenders or preferred shareholders. The more common ratios are given below.

### Security of current liabilities

$$\frac{\text{Net worth}}{\text{Current liabilities}}$$

This provides an indication of the protection which the creditors and short-term lenders are afforded. The higher the ratio, the more secure the current liabilities.

### Times interest earned

$$\frac{\text{Earnings before interest and taxes}}{\text{Debt interest}}$$

This ratio shows the number of times the earnings covers the debt interest. The higher the ratio, the greater the security of returns to lenders.

**Preferred dividend coverage**

$$\frac{\text{Earnings after taxes}}{\text{Preferred dividend requirement}}$$

This ratio provides an indication of the safety of preferred dividends. As before, the higher the ratio, the less likelihood there is of a preferred dividend being missed.

**Common shares**

A number of ratios are calculated which pay particular attention to shares, share values and dividends. The more common ratios calculated are as follows:

$$\text{Earnings per share} = \frac{\text{Net income after taxes and preferred dividends}}{\text{Number of shares outstanding}}$$

$$\text{Price–earnings ratio} = \frac{\text{Market price per share}}{\text{Earnings per share}}$$

$$\text{Dividends per share} = \frac{\text{Dividends to common shareholders}}{\text{Number of shares issued}}$$

$$\text{Dividend payout} = \frac{\text{Dividends}}{\text{Earnings}}$$

$$\text{Dividend yield} = \frac{\text{Dividends per share}}{\text{Market price per share}} \times 100$$

$$\text{Book value per share} = \frac{\text{Ordinary shareholders' equity}}{\text{Number of shares issued}}$$

## LIMITATIONS AND PROBLEMS OF RATIO ANALYSIS

**1.** Ratios are based on financial accounts, so they contain almost all of the deficiencies of these accounts.

**2.** Some ratios are open to manipulation and need to be interpreted with care, e.g., inventory levels may be kept artificially low at the year end, creating an impression of high efficiency in this area.

**3.** Inter-firm comparisons are faced with the problem that different organizations might use rather different accounting policies.

**4.** A financial analysis is particularly concerned with estimating the likely future flows of an organization. Traditional financial statements are not presented in the most appropriate form for such projection purposes, and some regrouping by types of flows is frequently needed, e.g., expenses may need to be split into those which are variable, quasi-fixed or fixed.

**5.** Detailed knowledge of a company's markets is seldom obtainable from the published accounts, yet such knowledge is particularly important for assessing future profitability.

**6.** Recognition of any cycles which relate to particular industries is important in forecasting. Short-term cyclical movements may well override long-term trends and must be built into forecasts.

**7.** Ratios are useful when comparing similar organizations operating under similar conditions. Comparisons with different types of organization can be misleading.

**8.** There is a real danger that ratio analysis can lead to conclusions which are oversimplified, e.g., a high current assets ratio is seen as good, while high credit periods allowed to debtors are seen as bad. Very little attention is paid to determining optimal values for ratios, yet in practice some kind of balancing between various ratios must be done.

# Chapter 5

# Taxation

## THE IMPORTANCE OF TAX IN FINANCIAL MANAGEMENT

Taxes on business profits are levied at such high rates, both in the US and most other Western economies, that to regard them as just an "irritating afterthought" is not enough. Management must assess the effect that tax will have on each possible course of action, in advance of any decisions being made. This approach is particularly important in investment and financing decisions as different methods frequently give rise to different tax treatment.

Given the aim of the book, this chapter will concentrate on an examination of the US tax system as it affects the activities of corporations, with particular emphasis on the **impact of tax on decisions concerned with investment and financing**. However, for purposes of completeness, a brief review of the taxation of individuals and unincorporated businesses is included in the last section of the chapter.

## ORDINARY INCOME AND CAPITAL GAINS

Companies trading in the US are subject to **corporate tax** on:

1. ordinary income;
2. capital gains.

**Ordinary income** may broadly be defined as the excess of sales revenue for a given period over the costs associated with the earning of those sales revenues.

**Capital gains** are defined as profits from the sale of capital assets; these are assets outside of the firm's ordinary business. The most common capital assets are investments in securities. Capital gains are classified as **short term** if the asset is held for less than one year and are taxed as ordinary income. Capital gains are classified as **long term** if the asset is held over one year and are taxed at the long-term capital gains rate, which is usually lower than the tax rate on ordinary income.

Ordinary income and capital gains are, effectively, taxed at different rates.

## CORPORATE TAX RATES

The tax rates for corporations and individuals are set by Congress and thus are subject to change over time. Congress established a five-tier corporate tax schedule for ordinary corporate earnings in the Revenue Act of 1978. The

**current tax rates for ordinary income**, established in the Economic Recovery Act of 1981, are given below.

| Corporate earnings | Tax rate |
|---|---|
| 0 – $25 000 | 15% |
| $25 001 – $50 000 | 18% |
| $50 001 – $75 000 | 30% |
| $75 001 – $100 000 | 40% |
| >$100 000 | 46% |

The first four increments of $25 000 are taxed at increasing rates; after $100 000 the incremental tax rate is 46%. The effective tax rate for large corporations is nearly the maximum incremental rate, 46%.

**Example:** A corporation with a taxable net income of $1 million would calculate its tax liability as follows: the first $100 000 would be taxed at the appropriate marginal rates; the remainder would be taxed at the 46% rate.

| Amount | × | Tax rate | = | Tax due |
|---|---|---|---|---|
| $25 000 | × | 0.15 | = | $3750 |
| $25 000 | × | 0.19 | = | $4750 |
| $25 000 | × | 0.30 | = | $7500 |
| $25 000 | × | 0.40 | = | $10 000 |
| $900 000 | × | 0.46 | = | $414 000 |
| Total taxes due | | | = | $440 000 |

The average tax rate for the corporation is 44%, which is nearly the marginal tax rate for income over $100 000.

**Capital gains from the sale of assets held less than one year are taxed as ordinary income.** If an asset is held over one year, it qualifies as a **long-term capital gain** and would be **taxed at a 28%** rate if corporate earnings exceed $50 000. If the earnings of the corporation are less than $50 000, long-term capital gains are treated as ordinary income (until the total income reaches $50 000) and therefore taxed at a lower rate.

For most large corporations the tax rate on capital gains is much less than the tax rate on ordinary income. For example, if a corporation's marginal tax rate on ordinary income is 46%, then its capital gains will be taxed at a 28% rate, which is 18% less than the rate on ordinary income.

**Example:** A corporation with taxable ordinary net income of $30 000 and taxable long-term capital gains of $30 000 would pay taxes as follows:

Tax on ordinary income less than $25 000
= 0.15 × $25 000 = $3750

Tax on ordinary income between $25 000 and $50 000
$= 0.18 \times \$5000 = \$900$

Tax on proportion of capital gains with total income less than $50 000
$= 0.18 \times \$20 000 = \$3600$

Tax on portion of capital gains with total income over $50 000
$= 0.28 \times \$10 000 = \$2800$

Total taxes due
$= \$11 300$

If ordinary earnings were greater than $50 000, the tax on long-term capital gains would be $0.28 \times \$30 000 = \$8400$.

## PAYMENT DATES

Corporations pay taxes during the current year based on the estimate of their earnings for the year which is reported to the IRS. At the end of the year the taxes are adjusted to reflect the **actual** earnings of the firm for the year. Unless the earnings estimates are equal to the previous year's earnings, or at least 80% of the current year's **actual** earnings, a penalty is imposed. Corporate taxes are paid in four equal installments on April 15, June 15, September 15 and December 15 of each year.

The firm must file a **final income statement** for the previous year's income by **March 15**. If the earnings estimate for the previous year was too low, the taxes on the **difference** are due on this date. If the earnings estimate was too large, the firm will receive a refund for the excess taxes paid.

## DETERMINATION OF TAXABLE NET INCOME

Ordinary income is taxed on the basis of the **net** income after interest expense shown in the company's income statement.

Direct costs of doing business are expensed in the income statement. Other items that are not a direct expense of doing business are deducted from the firm's revenues. These include depreciation, loss carry-forwards, and charitable contributions.

## TREATMENT OF DEPRECIATION

Corporations invest in many assets that are used for more than one year. Some of these assets can be treated as an expense in the year they are incurred, e.g., the purchase of a typewriter. Other assets are clearly long term and cannot be treated as an expense for the year they are incurred, e.g., a building with a useful life of 30 years.

The US tax system attempts to match the tax expense of an

asset with the time the "cost" (decrease in value of the asset) is incurred. This is accomplished by allowing the corporation to depreciate the value of the asset over its useful life.

Depreciation is treated as an expense; its effect is to reduce reported earnings. This reduces taxes paid by the firm and increases cash available to the firm.

**Example:** Consider the income and cash flow statements below. Both firms have the same sales revenue and operating costs. Firm A does not have depreciation to expense; firm B has a depreciation expense for the year of $20000.

|  | Firm A | Firm B |
|---|---|---|
| **Income Statement** |  |  |
| Sales | $100000 | $100000 |
| Costs (not including depreciation) | $50000 | $50000 |
| Depreciation | $0 | $20000 |
| Earnings before taxes | $50000 | $30000 |
| Taxes at 50% | $25000 | $15000 |
| Earnings after taxes | $25000 | $15000 |
| **Cash Flow Statement** |  |  |
| Sales | $100000 | $100000 |
| Cost (not including depreciation) | $50000 | $50000 |
| Taxes paid | $25000 | $15000 |
| After tax cash flow | $25000 | $35000 |

Firm A reports higher earnings, but it pays more in taxes and therefore has less cash available after taxes. Firm B's accounting earnings are $10000 less than firm A's, but its after-tax cash flow is $10000 more. In Chapter 6 we show that the cash generated from an investment is the best measure of its performance. After all, you cannot spend an income statement.

This reduction in taxes is known as the **depreciation tax shield**. The tax shield can be calculated by multiplying the amount of the depreciation deduction by the tax rate. In the above example the depreciation deduction is $20000 and the tax rate is 50%; therefore the depreciation tax shield is $20000 \times 0.5 = $10000.

In practice, depreciation is an arbitrary method of allocating the original cost of an asset over the life of the asset. The depreciation schedules for assets are designed to reflect the government's economic policy as well as the cost of using the asset over time. The government determines the **depreciable life** (the minimum life over which the asset can be depreciated) and the **depreciation schedule** (the allocation of the original cost over time) that is used. If the government wants to stimulate the economy, it may allow more generous depreciation treatment of investments. This lower tax liability increases the amount of cash available to businesses for investment and decreases the cost of investments for the firm.

A number of depreciation methods may be used: **straight line**, **units of production**, **sum of years' digits**, and **double declining balance**. The last two depreciation methods are known as **accelerated depreciation methods**, because they allow more of the depreciable cost of an asset to be deducted in the early years of its life.

**Straight line depreciation** allocates equal portions of the depreciable cost of the asset to each year of its depreciable life. The **depreciable cost** of an asset is its original cost less its salvage value. The **salvage value** of an asset is the amount that would be received from the sale of the asset at the end of its life.

$$\text{Annual straight line depreciation expense} = \frac{\text{Cost of the asset} - \text{salvage value}}{\text{Depreciable life of the asset}}$$

**Example:** A firm purchases a machine for $1 million; the useful life of the machine is 15 years; the depreciable life of the machine is 10 years. The firm uses straight line depreciation. In this case the salvage value of the asset is 0. The annual depreciation expense for the machine is:

$$\text{Annual depreciation expense} = \frac{\$1\,000\,000}{10 \text{ years}} = \$100\,000 \text{ per year}$$

If the company is taxed at a 46% rate, the depreciation expense of the machine reduces the company's taxes by $46000 (0.46 × $100000) each year.

If the project in which the machine is used has an expected life of 5 years, and the salvage value of the machine was $200000, the annual depreciation expense for that machine would be:

$$\text{Annual depreciation expense} = \frac{\$1\,000\,000 - \$200\,000}{5 \text{ years}} = \$160\,000$$

**Units of production depreciation** allocates the depreciable cost of an asset by the number of units of output the asset produces in the year, divided by the total number of units the asset is expected to produce over its life.

$$\text{Proportion of depreciable cost allocated to the year} = \frac{\text{Units of output for year}}{\text{Expected number of units of output over the life of the asset}}$$

**Example:** A machine costs $100000 and has a useful life of

4 years. The total output of the machine is expected to be 50 000 units. The number of units produced in each year is given below.

| Year | 1 | 2 | 3 | 4 |
|---|---|---|---|---|
| Units of output | 15 000 | 15 000 | 10 000 | 10 000 |

The depreciation expense for the first year is:

$$\text{Depreciation expense} = \$100\,000 \times \frac{15\,000}{50\,000} = \$30\,000$$

The annual depreciation expense over the life of the machine given below.

| Year | 1 | 2 | 3 | 4 |
|---|---|---|---|---|
| Depreciation expense | $30 000 | $30 000 | $20 000 | $20 000 |

**Sum of the years' digits depreciation** allocates the depreciable cost of an asset over the depreciable **life** of the asset. This is based on the number of years remaining in the asset's life divided by the sum of the years' digits of the asset's life. We will use the machine from the above example to illustrate this method.

First the sum of the digits for the depreciable life of the assets is calculated. For a life of 4 years this is $(1 + 2 + 3 + 4) = 10$.

The proportion of the depreciable value of the asset depreciated in each year is the number of years remaining in the asset's life divided by the sum of the years' digits. The depreciation expense for the first year of the machine is:

$$\text{Depreciation expense} = \$100\,000 \times \frac{4}{10} = \$40\,000$$

The depreciation charges over the life of the asset are:

| Year | 1 | 2 | 3 | 4 |
|---|---|---|---|---|
| Depreciation expense | $40 000 | $30 000 | $20 000 | $10 000 |

**Double declining balance** specifies that the depreciation expense for an asset is twice the straight line depreciation rate times the remaining balance of the original cost of the asset. At some point in the life of the asset, the depreciation charges using straight line depreciation (based on the depreciable cost of the asset) are greater than by using double declining balance; at this point convert to straight line depreciation. This point is determined by trial and error.

**Example:** A machine which costs $1 million will be used for 8 years, at which time it will be sold for $50 000. The straight line depreciation rate is 0.13, therefore the double declining balance depreciation rate is 0.26. The depreciation schedule for the machine is given below.

| Year | Balance | Double declining balance depreciation | Check for straight line depreciation |
|------|---------|---------------------------------------|--------------------------------------|
| 1 | $1 000 000 | $260 000 | |
| 2 | $740 000 | $192 400 | |
| 3 | $574 600 | $142 380 | |
| 4 | $432 220 | $112 380 | |
| 5 | $319 840 | $83 160 | $67 460 |
| 6 | $236 680 | $61 520 | $62 230 |
| 7 | $175 160 | $45 540 | |
| 8 | $129 620 | $33 700 | |

The depreciation charge for years 1 to 5 is determined by multiplying the balance column by 0.26. The balance for the next year is the previous year's balance less the depreciation charge. In years 5 and 6 we test to see if the depreciation charges for straight line depreciation are greater than those using double declining balance. This occurs in year 6. The depreciation charge for years 6, 7 and 8 is $62 230. This was determined by using straight line depreciation with a salvage value of $50 000 and the balance from year 6.

## TREATMENT OF THE SALE OF DEPRECIABLE ASSETS

When a depreciable asset is sold, the taxes due depend on the amount received from the sale, the original cost of the asset and the book value of the asset. If the amount received from the sale of the asset is **greater** than its original cost, this difference is taxed as a capital gain; the difference between the original cost and the book value of the asset is taxed as ordinary income. If the asset is sold for **less** than its original cost, the difference between the amount received and the book value is treated as a gain or loss of ordinary income. This prevents firms from converting ordinary income to capital gains by using accelerated depreciation methods.

**Example:** A firm sells a machine for $40 000. The original cost of the machine was $60 000 and the book value at the time of the sale was $30 000. The gain from the sale ($40 000 − $30 000 = $10 000) is taxed as ordinary income.

If the machine were sold for $70 000, there would be a taxable long-term capital gain of $70 000 − $60 000 = $10 000 and taxable ordinary income of $60 000 − $30 000 = $30 000 as a result of the sale.

Buildings are the exception to the above rule. The difference between the amount received and the book value, using straight line depreciation, is treated as a capital gain. If an accelerated depreciation method was used, the differ-

ence between the straight line depreciation book value and
the accelerated depreciation book value is taxed as ordinary
income.

## INVESTMENT TAX CREDIT

To stimulate business investment, Congress passed laws
allowing a percentage of new investments in long-term
assets to be credited against the corporation's income tax
liability. Under the rules in the 1978 tax law, 10% of the
investment for an asset with a life of 7 years or more may be
credited to the corporation's taxes. For investments with
lives of 5 or 6 years, a $6^2/_3$% tax credit is given. For investments with lives of 3 or 4 years, a $3^1/_3$% tax credit is given.

**Example:** A firm invests $1 million in an asset which
qualifies for an investment tax credit and has a useful life of
10 years. The asset qualifies for a 10% investment tax credit,
therefore the firm's tax liability for the year is reduced by
$0.1 \times \$1\,000\,000 = \$100\,000$.

## DIVIDEND EXCLUSIONS

Corporations are allowed to exclude 85% of the dividends
they receive from their taxable income. The remaining 15%
of the dividends are taxed as ordinary income. Since
dividends are paid from a corporation's after-tax earnings,
this dividend exclusion reduces the degree of double taxation on the earnings that generated the dividends.

**Example:** A firm with $100 000 in dividend income would
be taxed as though it had $0.15 \times \$100\,000 = \$15\,000$ of
ordinary income. The remaining $85 000 in dividends is not
taxed.

## TREATMENT OF LOSSES

If a company suffers a loss, the loss may be used to offset
taxable income. This is known as **carry-over**. Since they are
taxed at a lower rate than ordinary income, capital losses
cannot be used to offset ordinary income.

Losses may be used to offset past taxes, i.e., the IRS will
refund the taxes paid on past income that has been offset by
a current loss. This is called **carry-back**. Losses may also be
used to offset future earnings; this is called **carry-forward**.
Carry-back and carry-forward can be applied for a limited
number of years. Losses of ordinary income can be carried
back 3 years and forward for 7 years. Capital losses can be
carried back 3 years and forward for 5 years.

**Example:** A firm has a $10 000 loss in the current year. The
year before it had a taxable income of $1 million. The firm
can carry-back the loss, i.e., reduce the previous year's
income by $10 000 and receive a refund from the taxes paid

in the previous year. In this case the refund would be $0.46 \times$ $\$10\,000 = \$4600$.

The ability to carry over losses is valuable. A corporation with large profits could reduce its tax liability by acquiring a firm with large tax loss carry-forwards that are not offset by earnings. The tax code has been changed to reduce the incentives for this type of merger.

## DEDUCTIBILITY OF INTEREST

The tax code allows corporations to deduct the interest paid on its debt. This reduces the cost of debt for the corporation. For example, if a company borrows $\$1$ million in perpetuity at a 10% interest rate, it must pay its lenders $\$100\,000$ a year in interest. The cost of the debt to the corporation is not $\$100\,000$ since the company deducts the interest from its revenue in calculating its taxable net income. If the company's tax rate is 46%, the tax liability is reduced by $\$46\,000$, so that the after tax cost of the debt is $\$54\,000$. In Chapter 11 we discuss the implications of the tax deductibility of interest payments on a corporation's capital structure.

## PERSONAL TAX RATES

The tax rates for individuals' earned income increase from 0% to 50% as income increases. The personal tax structure has a **higher maximum rate than the corporate structure and increases at a faster rate.**

The **capital gains** tax rate for individuals is 40% of their marginal earned income tax rate. An individual with a marginal tax rate of 50% would have a $50\% \times 0.4 = 20\%$ tax rate on capital gains.

A number of items is deductible from personal income. These include: state and local taxes, interest, charitable contributions, losses from business operations and medical expenses. Individuals who do not itemize these expenses are allowed a standard lump-sum deduction. In addition to the above deductions, taxpayers are allowed to deduct $\$1000$ for each dependant. This deduction is doubled if the taxpayer is over 65 or blind.

**Earnings of sole proprietorships and partnerships are taxed as personal income.** This is true whether or not the earnings are distributed. At some point, the tax situation for retentions makes a corporate form more attractive than sole proprietorship or partnership, even though the distributed income will be taxed at both the corporate level and the individual level.

## PENALTIES ON EXCESSIVE RETAINED EARNINGS

Individuals with large incomes are taxed at higher rates than corporations. An individual could reduce his tax liability by creating a corporation to shelter income that he does not need, thus decreasing the amount of income subject to the higher personal tax rate. The tax code tries to prevent this by imposing penalties on corporations that retain excessive amounts of their earnings relative to their investment needs.

# Chapter 6

# Investment in Long-term Assets

## GENERAL APPROACH

An investment typically involves a relatively large **initial outflow of cash** which will then give rise to a series of **future inflows of cash**. The amounts of these inflows are often uncertain. The fact that large amounts of cash are committed for fairly long periods of time requires organizations to exercise considerable care in identifying possible projects and in selecting those projects which are to be undertaken.

Organizations should establish good, reliable systems for the identification of possible projects. This will involve constant research into the following.

**1.** The market.
**2.** New products.
**3.** New production methods.

Not all projects that are identified can be implemented, for a variety of reasons, and, therefore, an organization must select those which are both viable and beneficial to the firm. In choosing among projects, some formal appraisal techniques must be applied to each possibility and only those projects which pass the test should be undertaken. This chapter is particularly concerned with a consideration of the most important **methods of investment appraisal** and the efficiency of these methods.

Before we evaluate a project, the following information must be determined.

**1. All cash flows** relating to a project should be taken into account.

**2.** The **timing** of these flows should be considered.

**3. All relevant information** should be included (and, by the same token, all irrelevant information should be ignored).

## Appraisal methods

Any method chosen must be **practical and easy** to use. In general, several methods may be used to capture the benefits and risks that each project offers, though it must be clear to management what criteria were used in the choice of projects.

A wide variety of appraisal methods are used in practice with differing degrees of sophistication. The most commonly used methods are given below.

1. **Accounting rate of return** (ARR).
2. **Payback** (PBP).
3. **Net present value** (NPV).
4. **Internal rate of return** (IRR).

Each of these methods is described below. To help in the explanation and assessment process the following example will be used.

**Example** A firm is faced with buying either one of two labor-saving machines. The estimated data concerning the machines are as follows.

|  | Machine A ($) | Machine B ($) |
|---|---|---|
| Initial investment (Year 0) | 10000 | 10000 |
| Salvage value of machines (Year 5) | 2000 | 3000 |
| Annual labor cost savings: |  |  |
|   Year 1 | 4000 | 2000 |
|   Year 2 | 4000 | 3000 |
|   Year 3 | 4000 | 5000 |
|   Year 4 | 2000 | 7000 |
|   Year 5 | 2000 | 2000 |

The cost of funds raised for the initial investment will be 10% per annum over the life of the project (5 years). The annual cost savings will occur at the end of the year to which they relate. (This is a simplifying assumption which can be easily modified to suit different circumstances.)

**Accounting rate of return (ARR)**
With this method the accounting profit for the project is estimated and expressed as a percentage of the initial investment. The **decision rule** is that all projects which are expected to yield an ARR above a predetermined required rate of return are undertaken. Where mutually exclusive projects are competing, the one with the larger ARR is normally selected.

In applying ARR to the **example** given above, we must first convert the cash inflows into accounting profits associated with the project. This requires the identification of the appropriate depreciation figure to be deducted from cash flows. Straightline depreciation is calculated as the initial cost less **salvage value,** divided by the life of the project in years, i.e.

($10000 − $2000)/5 = $1600 for machine A.
($10000 − $3000)/5 = $1400 for machine B.

The accounting profits are defined as Cash flow − Depreciation.

| Accounting Profits | Machine A ($) | Machine B ($) |
|---|---|---|
| Year 1 | 2400 | 600 |
| Year 2 | 2400 | 1600 |
| Year 3 | 2400 | 3600 |
| Year 4 | 400 | 5600 |
| Year 5 | 400 | 600 |
| Average accounting profit | 1600 | 2400 |
| Average ARR on original investment | 16% | 24% |

On the basis of ARR, machine B would be chosen.

## Advantages of ARR

**1.** It takes account of all cash flows.
**2.** It is practical and straightforward to use.
**3.** Its results are understood by managers *provided* that they understand the basis of accounting profit.

## Disadvantages of ARR

**1.** It ignores the *timing* of cash flows. In the above example, if the *total* savings were the same, the same result would be obtained irrespective of *when* the savings occurred.

**2.** It takes account of certain information with respect to accounting adjustments (e.g., depreciation), which may then lead to an incorrect decision being made.

## Payback period (PBP)

This approach identifies the length of time it takes for the expected cash inflows to cover the initial investment. The **decision rule** is that only projects with shorter lives than a predetermined minimum are selected. If projects are competing, then the project with the shorter life is chosen. Applying this method to the **example** above gives the following payback periods.

Machine A    3 years
Machine B    3 years

In both cases, it will take three years to recover the original $10,000 invested. Proceeds occurring after the payback period are ignored.

On the basis of PBP, the two machines rank equally. However, note that if cash inflows were spread *evenly* over each year instead of being receivable at the year end, as is currently assumed, the payback periods would be as follows.

Machine A    2.5 years
Machine B    3 years

Machine A, then, would be preferred.

**Advantages of PBP**

**1.** It is practical and simple to use.

**2.** It is easy to understand.

**3.** Payback emphasizes the *short* term and so is likely to lead to fairly safe projects being chosen, particularly since it implicitly emphasizes liquidity.

**Disadvantages of PBP**

**1.** It ignores all cash flows *after* the payback period.

**2.** It does not take *timing* into account. Even within the payback period, timing is ignored; for machine B the payback period would have been the same (three years) even if the $5000 saving of Year 3 and the $2000 saving of Year 1 had been reversed.

### Net present value (NPV)

With this method, the timing of cash flows is implicitly taken into account. It must be recognized that cash flows of different periods cannot be compared directly since $1 now is not the equivalent of $1 receivable at a later date. The $1 could be reinvested to earn *interest,* such that it would accumulate to a greater sum in the future. The $1 held at present, and reinvested at 10%, would accumulate to $1.10 in one year's time, and to $1.21 in two years' time. In making comparisons between cash flows at different times, adjustments need to be made for this **time value of money**. The NPV method does so. It should be noted that this adjustment is *separate from any adjustment made for inflation.*

In bringing cash flows of different time periods to a common base, a base time-period needs to be determined. Since most investment decisions require outflows at an early stage of a project, followed by inflows at later stages, cash flows are usually expressed in terms of **present values**, i.e., amounts adjusted to values at the time that the decision is made. Future cash flows will, therefore, need to be *reduced* in order to calculate the amount which would need to be invested *now* to accumulate (by the addition of interest) to the expected future cash flow. This process is known as *discounting,* and the NPV method of investment appraisal is therefore known as a technique of **discounted cash flow**.

The present value (PV) of a cash flow occurring after one year can be calculated as follows.

$$PV = \frac{A}{(1 + k)} \text{ or } PV(1+k) = \text{Future value in 1 year}$$

where  A is the amount of the future cash flow,
       k is the interest (or discount) rate to be used.

Hence the present value of $1 received in one year's time, assuming an interest/discount rate of 10%, is:

$$PV = \frac{\$1}{(1 + 0.10)} = \frac{\$1}{1.10} = \$0.91$$

The present value calculation can be generalized to cover any period as follows.

$$PV = \frac{A_n}{(1 + k)^n}$$

where $A_n$ is the amount of the future cash flow in the given period,
$k$ is the interest (or discount) rate to be used,
$n$ is the time lapse between now and the cash flow.

From the above calculations it should be clear that the larger the discount rate ($k$) and the longer the time lapse ($n$), the smaller the PV becomes.

In practice, it is not necessary to calculate PVs from first principles, as tables are widely available which give the PV of $1 discounted at a range of discount rates over a number of time periods. Examples are given in the appendices on page 118.

The NPV method operates by discounting all future cash flows to PVs and then comparing the total of the PVs of the cash inflows with those of the cash outflows. The **decision rule** is that those projects where the PV of the inflows exceeds that of the outflows (i.e., those which have a positive net present value) are adopted. Those with a negative net present value (NPV) are rejected. Where there are competing projects, the one with the larger positive NPV will normally be chosen.

Applying the NPV method to the **example** on page 52 we get:

| | Machine A | | | Machine B | | |
|---|---|---|---|---|---|---|
| Year | Cash flow | Discount factor | PV | Cash flow | Discount factor | PV |
| 0 | -10 000 | 1.0 | -10 000 | -10 000 | 1.0 | -10 000 |
| 1 | 4 000 | 0.909 | 3 636 | 2 000 | 0.909 | 1 818 |
| 2 | 4 000 | 0.826 | 3 304 | 3 000 | 0.826 | 2 478 |
| 3 | 4 000 | 0.751 | 3 004 | 5 000 | 0.751 | 3 755 |
| 4 | 2 000 | 0.683 | 1 366 | 7 000 | 0.683 | 4 781 |
| 5 | 4 000 | 0.621 | 2 484 | 5 000 | 0.621 | 3 105 |
| Net present value | | | $3 794 | | | $5 937 |

The discount factors are obtained from the present value table in Appendix 1 on page 118. For the purpose of illustration, a 10% discount rate is used. The PV of a future cash flow is calculated by multiplying the cash flow for a period by the appropriate discount rate. The NPV is the sum of the individual PVs. The Year 5 cash flows include the proceeds from the sale of the depreciated asset (salvage value).

Both projects are acceptable when using the NPV approach. As they are **mutually exclusive**, machine B would be chosen since it gives the higher NPV.

## Advantages of NPV

**1.** *All* cash flows are included in the appraisal.

**2.** The *timing* of the cash flows is taken into account.

**3.** The method is not subject to the problems caused by accounting adjustments since decisions are based on cash flows.

**4.** It is fairly easy to use, although identification of the appropriate discount rate can be a problem.

## Disadvantages of NPV

**1.** The exact meaning of NPV is not readily obvious, and many businesses prefer to use rates of return.

**2.** The method of ranking projects by the size of the NPV can lead to incorrect decisions, where the following situations exist.

   (a) Constraints on the amount of funds available for capital projects.
   (b) Investment indivisibilities.

These problems are dealt with more fully in the book on *Management Accounting* in this series.

### NPV–another viewpoint
The meaning of NPV becomes more clear if we consider a project which is financed by a particular source of funds on which interest is to be paid. The discount rate can thus be viewed as the cost of funds. An NPV of zero would mean that cash inflows are sufficient to cover both the cash outflows and the associated interest. Hence, an NPV of zero means that the project is earning a return equal to the discount rate used.

### Internal rate of return (IRR)
This method–also referred to as the **yield method**–is closely related to the NPV approach since it is also based on the discounted cash flow technique (DCF). It is the rate of return earned by a project.

Following the logic of the last section, the IRR is the discount rate which, when applied to a project's cash flows, gives a zero NPV. The **decision rule** is that all projects whose IRR exceeds the cost of capital should be undertaken. If all projects cannot be undertaken, the project with the higher IRR is normally chosen.

For a simple accept or reject decision regarding a project, both NPV and IRR should give the same result.

**1.** With NPV, projects should be accepted when they give a positive value, when cash flows are discounted at the cost of funds.

**2.** With IRR, projects should be accepted when they give a return in excess of the cost of funds.

If the same cost of funds is used in both calculations, the above are *identical* decision rules. A project, which when discounted at the cost of funds gives a positive NPV, *must* be giving a return in excess of the discount rate used. One which gives a negative NPV *must* be giving a return of less than the discount rate used.

**Calculation of the IRR** requires a trial and error approach. This can be seen if we apply the method to the **example**.

**Machine A** As this project has a positive NPV when discounted at 10% (see solution using NPV on page 55), then the IRR must be greater than 10%.

For the first trial a 20% discount rate will be used.

| Year | Cash flow ($) | Discount factor | PV ($) |
|------|------|------|------|
| 0 | −10000 | 1.0 | −10000 |
| 1 | 4000 | 0.833 | 3332 |
| 2 | 4000 | 0.694 | 2776 |
| 3 | 4000 | 0.579 | 2316 |
| 4 | 2000 | 0.482 | 964 |
| 5 | 4000 | 0.402 | 1608 |

| NPV at 20% discount rate | $996 |
|------|------|

As the NPV is still positive, the IRR is greater than 20%.

In practice, a number of calculations of this type can be made to determine the exact return, which in the above case is between 24% and 25%. Such calculations are frequently computerized.

For examination purposes, **approximations** can be made either arithmetically or graphically. With the graphical method the NPVs calculated (at 10% and 20% in our example) are plotted against the discount rate, and the IRR can be derived by interpolation or extrapolation. An example is given in Figure 1.

Alternatively, an approximate figure can be calculated arithmetically as follows.

$
NPV at 10%  +  3794
NPV at 20%  +   996

Therefore a 10% increase in the discount rate gives a decrease in NPV of $2798.

Therefore a 1% increase in the discount rate gives a decrease in NPV of approximately $280.

The IRR is the rate at which NPV is zero, so the discount factor needs to increase by approximately 4%, giving an IRR of 24%.

It must be recognized that both approaches assume linear relationships which do not in fact exist, and small errors may occur. These are unlikely to be significant for examination purposes.

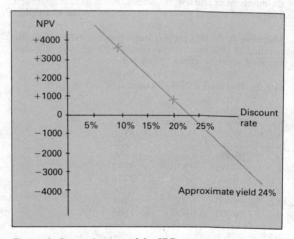

*Figure 1. Determination of the IRR*

**Machine B** It should be clear from the NPV calculations for the project that the IRR of machine B is above 10% and probably well above it.

Similar calculations can be made to those performed for machine A, giving an IRR of approximately 27%.

### Advantages of IRR

**1.** *All* cash flows are included in the calculations.

**2.** The *timing* of the cash flows is taken into account.

**3.** The method is not subject to the problems caused by accounting adjustments since decisions are based on cash flows.

**4.** The results of the appraisal are expressed in a form which is acceptable to, and understandable by, managers.

### Disadvantages of IRR

**1.** IRR is more difficult to calculate, although the increased availability of computer packages means that this is no longer a real problem.

**2.** Some projects with certain cash flow characteristics can have more than one IRR, frequently of very different magnitudes.

**3.** The IRR method assumes that all cash flows are reinvested at the IRR, an assumption rarely borne out in practice.

**4.** IRR has a number of weaknesses when it comes to choosing between projects, and is generally considered to be less satisfactory than NPV. In particular, a small project may be chosen in preference to a large one because it has a higher IRR, but the NPV of the larger project may be very much larger, and the larger project should, therefore, be chosen. In fact, both NPV and yield need to be applied with care when choosing between projects, particularly where constraints operate on the amounts to be invested or where projects are not divisible. (This area is dealt with in more detail in the *Management Accounting* book published in this series.)

### Conclusions on appraisal methods

The above analysis of the appraisal methods commonly used clearly suggests that those methods based on discounted cash flow techniques are the most effective. This is supported by recent research findings which suggest that managers in industry and commerce are tending to move away from ARR and PBP and towards DCF methods.

It should be noted, however, that the various methods are not necessarily to be perceived as alternatives, and the use of **more than one method of appraisal** has distinct advantages. The use of both DCF and PBP seems to be the most popular combination of methods.

## APPRAISAL METHODS, BUSINESS OBJECTIVES AND THE THEORY OF FINANCE

In an appraisal of the various methods, some consideration should be given to the assumptions being made, if any, about the objectives of the organization.

**1.** ARR would appear to be concerned with the **maximization of the accounting rate of return**.
**2.** PBP is concerned with objectives to do with **risk reduction**, particularly in the area of liquidity.
**3.** DCF techniques are based on the assumed objective of **maximization of shareholders' or owners' wealth**.

This last objective is the most commonly assumed objective in the various theories of finance put forward. When it is directly related to the NPV approach, the meaning of NPV can be further clarified.

For illustration purposes, let us refer back to machine A, which had a positive NPV of +$3794 when a discount rate of 10% was assumed. This implies that the owners of the firm could borrow $13794—which is the amount of the initial investment ($10000) plus the NPV ($3794)—and pay back this amount, with interest, from the cash inflows occurring.

This can be demonstrated as follows.

|  |  | $ |
|---|---|---|
| Year 0 initial borrowing |  | 13794 |
| Add: Interest for first year ($13794 @ 10%) |  | 1379 |
|  |  | 15173 |
| Less: Year 1 cash inflow |  | 4000 |
|  |  | 11173 |
| Add: Interest for 2nd year ($11173 @ 10%) |  | 1117 |
|  |  | 12290 |
| Less: Year 2 cash inflow |  | 4000 |
|  |  | 8290 |
| Add: Interest for 3rd year ($8290 @ 10%) |  | 829 |
|  |  | 9119 |
| Less: Year 3 cash inflow |  | 4000 |
|  |  | 5119 |
| Add: Interest for 4th year ($5119 @ 10%) |  | 512 |
|  |  | 5631 |
| Less: Year 4 cash inflow |  | 2000 |
|  |  | 3631 |
| Add: Interest for 5th year ($3631 @ 10%) |  | 363 |
|  |  | 3994 |
| Less: Year 5 cash inflow |  | 4000 |
|  |  | -$ 6 |

(The $6 difference shown above is due to rounding errors.)

The positive NPV ($3794) could thus be viewed as the **increment in wealth** that should accrue to the owners as a result of this particular project being taken on. The reason is, theoretically at least, the extra $3794 borrowed—over and above that needed for the investment—*could* be paid out to the owners immediately and repaid from the inflows associated with the project. The owners would thus immediately be better off to the extent of $3794. If the $3794 were retained within the organization, we would still expect to see an increase in owners' wealth of the same amount because of an increase in the value of the business. If the $3794 were not borrowed, the inflows would accumulate to a sum which exceeded the outflows with a present value of $3794. The result should therefore be the same.

Of course, in practice, events do not occur with the precision implied by the above logic. Detailed information of the type given above is not usually made available to those outside an organization and in addition cash flows are associated with a considerable amount of risk and uncertainty. However, these problems occur with any appraisal method, and the logic of the NPV approach is such that many of the theories of finance relating to such items as capital structure, dividend policy, etc., are based upon it, together with the assumed objective of maximization of shareholders' wealth.

## RISK AND UNCERTAINTY

### Techniques for dealing with risk
The discussion so far has been based on the assumption that the cash flows to be used in appraisal methods can be ascertained with certainty. In reality, such precision does not exist and decisions have to be made on less than perfect information. To date, no completely satisfactory methods of dealing with risks and uncertainty have been devised, but a number of techniques have been developed which help management to assess the size and nature of the risks involved. Such techniques may be considered to be **risk analysis** techniques and the more important of these are given below.

### 1. The bail-out facility of a project
In essence, this technique asks, "How much can be recovered if the project goes wrong at various stages of its life?" The higher the possible recovery, the lower are the real risks involved. It is clear, then, that investments in assets with high disposal values, or those which have a number of alternative uses, are much less risky than assets with low disposal values and a limited number of alternative uses.

### 2. The use of probabilities
For some projects returns are so uncertain that it is impossible to say exactly what the NPV of a project is. In some of these cases it is possible to estimate the likely spread or dispersion of results, and to attach probabilities to them. The use of probabilities enables estimates to be made of:

(a) the **expected value**;
(b) the **dispersion, or spread, of returns**.

The use of expected value (a weighted average) raises certain problems, as it may not be the most likely result.

Indeed, it may not even be a possible result, and knowledge of the dispersion of returns is of undoubted assistance in choosing between projects. For example, three projects are shown in Figure 2, all with the same expected (average) value but with different dispersions of possible returns. The correct decision is not clear and will depend upon management's attitudes towards risk and the overall portfolio of projects. However, in general terms, one would expect projects with a low spread of possible returns to be preferred to those with a high spread. A would thus normally be chosen in preference to B in the above situation. For this reason, the **variance** or **standard deviation** of possible returns is frequently calculated and used as a measure of risk.

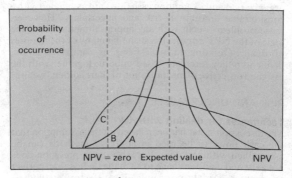

*Figure 2. Dispersion of returns*

### 3. Decision trees
In many investment projects critical points arise, at which times further decisions need to be made. Pilot studies or mini-versions of a project are frequently undertaken to test market reaction and assess problems. The results of these will then determine subsequent action. Demand conditions may vary, with expansion or contraction being required under certain of these conditions. Decision trees can help in clarifying such problems by mapping out the various alternatives or branches which exist, in sequence, and assessing the NPV and probability associated with each branch. An example is given in Figure 3.

### 4. Simulation
For complicated problems, simulation techniques are increasingly being used to assess risk, by analyzing large numbers of possible outcomes and bringing these together in the form of a probability distribution of NPV.

### 5. Sensitivity analysis
Sensitivity analysis is a technique used to determine which of the many variables in a particular project are the most critical to the success or failure of a project. In broad terms, sensitivity analysis asks the question, "What happens if we change one (or more) of the variables in the project?" The figures used as the basis of an appraisal are modified to take

into account changes in a number of variables, taken one at a time or jointly as required. In this way, management should be able to identify which variables are critical and ensure, where possible, that such variables are kept under close control. Variables which are commonly analyzed include sales volume, selling price, variable costs, project life, plant capacity, etc.

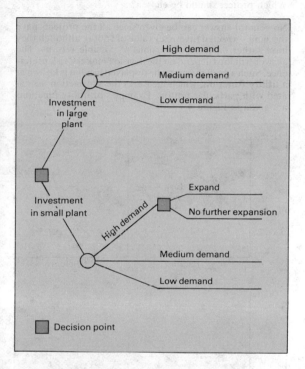

Investment in large plant
High demand
Medium demand
Low demand

Investment in small plant
High demand
Expand
No further expansion
Medium demand
Low demand

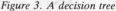
Decision point

*Figure 3. A decision tree*

The above list of techniques is not exhaustive, nor have these techniques been developed in any particularly systematic way. Nevertheless, the use of such techniques can assist considerably in identifying **areas of risk** and the **extent of the risks** actually taken.

## Management attitudes towards risk

It is important to recognize that the identification of risk does not of itself provide a decision rule, since attitudes towards risk vary tremendously. It is thus not possible to derive generalized decision rules. Nonetheless, effective decision making requires an understanding of risk preferences and attitudes towards risk.

**Example:** A choice has to be made between three projects:

Project A, which gives $5000 in one year's time, with certainty.
Project B, which gives a 50% chance of zero, and a 50% chance of $10000 in one year's time.
Project C, which gives a 20% chance of losing $2000, a 60% chance of receiving $5000, and a 20% chance of receiving $12000, all in one year's time.
Which project should be chosen?

No general answer can be given since all the projects have the same expected (average) value of $5000, although they have rather different dispersions of possible returns. The answer will thus depend on the decision makers' risk preference. Such a preference can be displayed in what is known as a **utility function**, which measures the satisfaction associated with particular returns. Examples of utility functions are given in Figure 4.

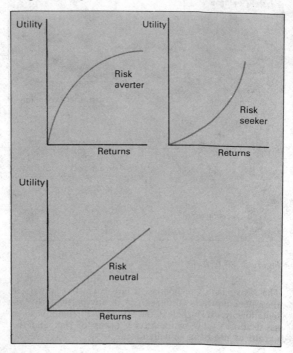

*Figure 4. Utility functions*

The risk averter attaches less marginal utility to increasing returns; the risk seeker is attracted by risk while the risk neutral investor attaches the same importance to all marginal returns. If the three projects referred to above are related to the three types of curve, we should find that the risk averse investor prefers A, the risk seeking investor prefers C, and the risk neutral investor is indifferent be-

tween the three. In fact, most people seem to be risk averse
and the majority of decisions reflect this.

Considerable doubt has been expressed as to the usefulness
of utility functions in practice. Very few examples exist of
practical applications of the concept to businesses.
Nevertheless, the above ideas are useful in understanding
the importance to the investment decision of attitudes
towards risk, and in explaining why particular choices are
made in practice. In particular, it explains why management
is usually unprepared to take on projects with even a small
known possibility of a sizeable loss, because of the disutility
associated with such projects.

Once risks have been identified, and attitudes towards them
have been clarified, a balanced decision should be possible.
However, in practice it is doubtful whether the steps and
techniques suggested above are used as widely as they might
be. It is more common to find rather **simpler methods**
being used to allow for risk, such as the following.

**1.** The use of a shortened payback period.
**2.** The use of a higher discount rate.

### Shortened payback period
It has already been pointed out that the use of payback tends
to lead to less risky projects being chosen. One common
response to risky projects is to require *even shorter* payback
periods: the problems associated with payback will still
remain but the risk of loss is considerably reduced. This is
closely related to the bail-out facility referred to earlier. The
shortened payback period method is not particularly useful
in dealing with projects where outcomes cannot be predicted with any degree of accuracy.

### Higher discount rate
It is quite common for management to decide that a higher
rate of return is needed on certain projects to compensate
for the higher risk associated with those projects. This is
consistent with the actions of many in the financial sector,
where required rates of return are frequently increased to
cover additional risk. It is nevertheless a somewhat hit-or-
miss approach as far as the individual organization is concerned.

### Portfolio effects and risk reduction
In some projects uncertainty can be reduced by the use of a
variety of techniques such as market research and market
sampling. Risk can be reduced by market samples, by the
use of projects whose capital assets maintain a high disposal
value (thus preserving more flexibility) and by project
diversification. Even where quite high risks are associated
with individual projects, it is possible for an organization to
reduce its overall risk profile by diversification, thus obtaining the benefits of a portfolio of projects. That is, by
undertaking several unrelated projects, a firm will reduce its
risk by not putting "all its eggs in one basket".

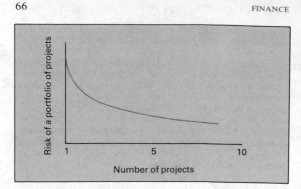

*Figure 5. Effect of Project Diversification*

Diversification reduces some of the project's risk – namely
the risk particular to a project. The risk that diversification
cannot eliminate is called *market* risk.

**Chapter 7**

# Security and Business Valuations

Business organizations tend to invest mainly in real assets—plant, machinery, inventory, etc.—although sometimes they invest in **financial assets**, namely securities issued by other organizations—both business and public sector organizations.

Possible **reasons for investing in financial assets** include the following:

**1.** The **objectives of certain organizations** (e.g., investment companies) may include investing partially or wholly in financial assets.

**2.** Investment in financial assets may be a practical means of **risk reduction** through **diversification**.

**3.** Financial assets provide a useful **revenue earning repository** for short-term cash surpluses. It should be noted that this is only likely to be true of securities which are actively traded, so the purchase and sale of such assets will be easily done.

**4.** Financial assets may be acquired in order **to obtain control** over the assets of another organization. Control can be achieved by obtaining sufficient ordinary shares to achieve voting control.

In addition to business organizations, a great many individuals and non-business organizations invest in financial assets, and the remaining sections of this chapter apply equally to them.

In broad terms, the same type of evaluation and appraisal techniques used for investment in real assets can be applied to financial assets. However, in practice, **discounted cash flow techniques (DCF)** are the most widely used, and the majority of the valuation models proposed follow this logic. The use of DCF requires some assessment of future cash flows, and the identification of an appropriate discount rate. Thus, the estimation of such things as future earnings, dividends, market values, taxation rates and changes therein, etc., must be seen as an essential part of the valuation process.

## PREDICTION OF FUTURE EVENTS AND RESULTS

This relies largely on information about:

**1.** the national economy;
**2.** the industry;
**3.** the particular organization concerned.

Estimates of the **likely future state of the economy** can be aided by information obtained from a variety of statistical sources, particularly government publications. The main economic trends need to be identified, along with additional factors such as productivity, employment, credit, balance of payments, price indices, etc. Many of the statistics used in this first part of the analysis will also provide extremely useful **industrial information**, and are likely to provide a basis for estimating market size, capital expenditure needs, likely cost escalation and profitability, etc.

Any **assessment of the individual organization** involves a detailed examination of past performance, the current situation and future prospects. This examination is likely to center on the analysis of past accounting information, in order to help in the prediction of future events; this topic has been dealt with in Chapter 4. However, past information is not always a reliable indicator of likely future performance, and other factors and sources of information need to be considered in conjunction with past information.

## SECURITY VALUATION–THE APPROACH TO THE PROBLEM

Once the returns from a security have been estimated, the valuation problem can be viewed as a discounted cash flow problem, with expected cash flows being discounted by the rate of return required by security holders.

The **required rate of return** is the minimum rate of return necessary to induce investors to buy or hold a security. It must be recognized that not all securities carry an equal risk. Thus, higher risk securities will need to yield higher returns than lower risk securities if investors are to invest in them. For any given risky security the required rate of return is equal to the **riskless rate** plus a **risk premium**. The current yield on government securities is normally taken to be the riskless rate. The relationship between risk and required return can be illustrated graphically as shown in Figure 6 and is known as the **securities market line**.

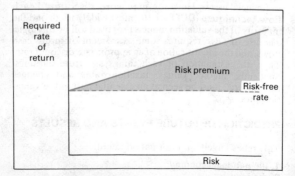

*Figure 6. The relationship between risk and return*

The figure illustrates the point that the required rate of return for a security with high risk will be higher than that for one with a lower risk.

Changes in the level of interest rates will change the riskless rate, so the line will move up and down by the amount of that change. Changes in investors' attitudes towards risk may result in changes in the slope of the line. If investors become more averse to risk, the line will become steeper, implying a higher required return for the same degree of risk. If they become less averse to risk, the line will become flatter.

## BOND VALUATION

### Perpetual bonds

Perpetual bonds are securities which pay a fixed amount of interest *indefinitely*, with no repayment of the capital sum outstanding. While not common in the US, the British government has issued perpetual bonds.

A bond of this type can be valued as follows.

$$PV = \frac{I}{(1+k)} + \frac{I}{(1+k)^2} + \ldots \frac{I}{(1+k)^n}$$

where I is the interest payable,
k is the required rate of return,
n is the remaining life of the security.

For a perpetuity (i.e., n = infinity) this reduces to:

$$PV = \frac{I}{k}$$

**Example** A perpetual bond issued for $100 pays $4 in annual interest. The current rate of interest on bonds of this type is 10%. The price for the bond is likely to be

$$PV = \frac{\$4}{0.10} = \$40.$$

Put another way, the acquisition of a 4% perpetuity bond at a price of $40 will give the market rate of return of 10%.

If the current interest rate was 6% one would expect the price to be

$$PV = \frac{\$4}{0.06} = \$66.60.$$

If the current rate of interest were 16% or 2% the figures would be $25 and $200 respectively.

From the above example it is apparent that **interest rate changes** are likely to have a significant effect on the price of perpetual bonds. However, it is unlikely that price changes would occur with the precision implied above, since these figures are based on permanent changes in the interest rate. Short-term changes in interest rates will only affect bond prices in the short run. Rather, it is the **expectations of the long-term interest rate** which is likely to be paramount.

### Fixed-term bonds

These are securities which pay interest, *and* repay the capital sum at some agreed future time.

A bond of this type can be valued as follows.

$$PV = \frac{I}{(1+k)} + \frac{I}{(1+k)^2} + \ldots + \frac{(I+M)}{(1+k)^n}$$

where I is the annual interest,
      M is the maturity value,
      k is the required rate of return,
      n is the remaining life of the bond.

**Example** What is the likely price for a government security (nominal value $100) paying 4% interest and redeemable by the government in four years' time, if the current rate of return is: 10%; 6%; 16%; 2%?

The value, assuming a **required rate of return of 10 %**, can be derived as follows.

$$PV = \frac{\$4}{(1+0.10)} + \frac{\$4}{(1+0.10)^2} + \frac{\$4}{(1+0.10)^3} + \frac{(\$4+\$100)}{(1+0.10)^4}$$
$$= (\$4 \times 0.909) + (\$4 \times 0.826) + (\$4 \times 0.75) + (\$104 \times 0.683)$$
$$= \$80.98$$

Similar calculations for the other three required rates of return give prices of $93.06 (6% return), $66.39 (16% return), and $107.65 (2% return).

Comparison of the prices calculated for different required rates of return for the perpetuity and the four-year bond indicates clearly that the longer the period to maturity of a security, the greater its price change in response to a given change in interest rates. This greater **interest rate risk** which is associated with perpetuities explains why short-term bonds usually have lower yields than long-term bonds, in spite of similar levels of confidence in the returns. It also explains the reluctance of most managers to hold their near-cash reserves in the form of long-term debt securities.

It should be noted that, so far, knowledge of the discount rate (i.e., the required rate of return) has been presumed, along with knowledge of future cash flows. This has enabled calculations to be made of the appropriate value of the security. If the value of the security were known, along with its associated cash flows, its yield could be calculated.

**Example:** Find the yield to maturity of a bond—currently

priced on the market at $80—with a par value of $100, an 8% coupon rate and which is redeemable in four years' time at a premium of 10%.

If the cash flows are discounted at 10% and 20% the following present values are obtained.

| | Cash flow ($) | (At 10%) Discount factor | PV ($) | (At 20%) Discount factor | PV ($) |
|---|---|---|---|---|---|
| Initial outflow | (80) | 1.0 | (80) | 1.0 | (80) |
| Inflows | | | | | |
| Year 1 | 8 | 0.909 | 7.27 | 0.833 | 6.66 |
| 2 | 8 | 0.826 | 6.61 | 0.694 | 5.56 |
| 3 | 8 | 0.751 | 6.00 | 0.579 | 4.63 |
| 4 | 118 | 0.683 | 80.59 | 0.482 | 56.88 |
| Net present value | | | +$20.47 | | −$6.27 |

By a process of interpolation the yield can be ascertained to be

$$10\% + \left( \frac{20.47}{26.74} \times 10\% \right) = 17.7\%$$

It is worth noting that the use of **annuity tables** (see Appendix II on page 118) can considerably reduce the amount of arithmetical calculation needed.

It should also be recognized that the techniques illustrated above can be applied to **preferred shares,** which have similar cash flow characteristics to fixed term bonds.

## VALUATION OF ORDINARY SHARES

In theory, the same ideas apply as in the last section. The value of a share *should be* the sum of future dividends, discounted at an appropriate rate, i.e.,

$$P = \frac{D_1}{(1+k)} + \frac{D_2}{(1+k)^2} + \frac{D_n}{(1+k)^3} + \ldots + \frac{D_n}{(1+k)^n}$$

where P = current value

D_n = dividends in period n,

k = required rate of return.

However, in practice several **difficulties** occur with share valuations, which pose problems for the above model.

**1.** The **degree of uncertainty** with regard to earnings, dividends and share prices.

**2.** Unlike loan interest and preferred dividends, ordinary dividends and share prices are usually **expected to grow**, thus making the application of standard formulae more difficult.

**3.** Rather different values will be given to shares, depending upon whether they are:

(a) **private** or **public** companies,
(b) **quoted** or **unquoted**.

**4.** In certain cases, the question arises as to whether a purchase of shares gives a **majority** (i.e., controlling) **holding** or a **minority holding**, resulting in possible differences in share values.

A number of **models or approaches to the valuation of ordinary shares** are given below. However, it must be recognized that share valuation is an *imprecise art,* and no perfect models have yet been put forward. A considerable amount of research has taken place over the years in an attempt to identify the factors which influence or explain share pricing. The **most common explanatory variables** include the following:

**1.** The level of earnings.
**2.** Expected growth in earnings.
**3.** The level of dividends and/or the dividend payout ratio.
**4.** Expected growth in dividends.
**5.** Historic share price variability.
**6.** Historic earnings variability.

Recent research has also suggested the following:

**1.** Some measure of correlation between earnings of the particular organization and those of the market.
**2.** A measure of leverage.
**3.** An index of operating asset liquidity.
**4.** A measure of firm size.

### Growth models
A model to incorporate growth can be developed as follows.

$$P_0 = \frac{D_1 + P_1}{(1+k)}$$

where $D_1$ is the dividend at the end of Year 1,
$P_1$ is the market price at the end of Year 1,
$P_0$ is the market price at the end of Year 0,
$k$ is the required rate of return.

Therefore $P_0 = \dfrac{D_1 + P_0(1+g)}{(1+k)} = \dfrac{D_1 + P_0 + P_0 g}{(1+k)}$

where $g$ is the expected growth rate in market price.

This reduces to $P_0 + P_0k = D_1 + P_0 + P_0g$.

Therefore $P_0k - P_0g = D_1$

$$P_0 = \frac{D_1}{(k - g)}$$

In applying this model to growth situations, it must be recognized that to be valid for more than one period a **constant growth rate must be assumed** in earnings, dividends and market price.

**Example:** Mr X is thinking of buying a share in the ABC Co. which he intends to hold for one year. An annual dividend of 50¢ per share has just been paid. Dividends have been growing at about 6% per annum for several years, and this rate is expected to continue. The current rate of return on riskless stocks is 10%, and Mr X considers that a risk premium of 4% is appropriate for an organization such as ABC Co.

How much should Mr X be prepared to pay for a share in ABC Co.

$$P_0 = \frac{D_1}{(k - g)}$$

where $D_1 = 53¢$,
$\phantom{where }k = 14\%\ (0.14)$,
$\phantom{where }g = \phantom{0}6\%\ (0.06)$.

Therefore $P_0 = \dfrac{53}{(0.14 - 0.06)} = \dfrac{53}{0.08} = \$6.63$.

In practice, organizations typically go through phases where growth occurs at rather different rates. In such a case the above approach can be modified to arrive at a present price.

**Example:** DEF Co. is expected to grow at a rate of about 20% for the next four years, then at 10% for the next three years and finally settle down to a growth rate of 5% for the indefinite future. The company's ordinary shares currently pay a dividend of 50¢ per share, but dividends are expected to increase in proportion to the growth of the firm.

What value should be placed on the ordinary shares if a 10% return is required?

Estimates of dividends can be made for the first two periods of growth, and these can be discounted at the required rate (10%) as shown below.

| Year | Dividends ($) | Discount factor | PV ($) |
|------|---------------|-----------------|--------|
| 1 | .60 | 0.909 | .54 |
| 2 | .72 | 0.826 | .59 |
| 3 | .86 | 0.751 | .65 |
| 4 | 1.04 | 0.683 | .71 |
| 5 | 1.14 | 0.621 | .71 |
| 6 | 1.26 | 0.564 | .71 |
| 7 | 1.38 | 0.513 | .71 |
| | | | $4.62 |

At the beginning of Year 8 a period of constant annual growth (5%) is entered. The shares could thus be expected to be valued at:

$$P = \frac{D_8}{(k-g)} = \frac{\$1.45^*}{(0.10-0.05)} = \$28.98$$

*i.e., $(1.38 + 5\%)$.

This value is calculated as at the beginning of Year 8 (which is taken to be the end of Year 7 for discounting purposes). Its present value is thus $28.98 \times 0.513 = \$14.86$.

An ordinary share in DEF. Co. should thus be valued at $19.48 (i.e., $14.86 + $4.62).

## Market yields and multipliers
Over the years a number of factors have been used by the market to identify important relationships. The two most common factors are:

1. the **dividend yield**;
2. the **price-earnings ratio**.

The method of calculation for each is given below.

$$\text{Dividend yield} = \frac{\text{Dividends per share}}{\text{Market price per share}} \times 100$$

$$\text{Price-earnings ratio} = \frac{\text{Share price}}{\text{Earnings per share}}$$

Securities in similar risk categories are likely to have similar ratios, and estimates of share price can be made by applying these market figures to dividends or earnings.

**Example:** An organization has annual profits after tax of $1m, and 2 million $1 shares. If an investor regards a PE ratio of 10 as appropriate to such a share—taking risk and other factors into account—what value would be placed on each share?

$$\text{Earnings per share} = \frac{\$1m}{2m} = \$.50$$

$$\text{If PE ratio} = \frac{\text{Share price}}{\text{Earnings per share}}$$

then share price = PE ratio × earnings per share

$$= 10 \times \$.50$$

$$= \$5 \text{ per share}$$

High PE ratios tend to be associated with organizations with perceived growth prospects.

### Private/public – quoted/unquoted

In valuing shares, differences are likely to arise because of the ease (or otherwise) of **transferability of shares**. Private companies usually impose restrictions on the rights of shareholders to transfer their shares and so are generally regarded as more risky than public companies in that finding a buyer for unwanted shares may be difficult. Similarly, if an organization's securities are listed on a stock exchange, these securities can be disposed of much more quickly and easily than those of an unlisted firm, and this will have an effect on share prices.

### Majority/minority holdings

The value which an investor places on a share is also likely to be influenced by whether he acquires:

**1.** a minority holding;

**2.** a majority holding.

The price set for the acquisition of a **minority holding** is likely to be largely determined by the **dividend yield** since, in practical terms, such a holding does not give the shareholder any opportunity to influence future decisions. The investment decision will thus probably have to be based upon expectations about future dividends. Acquisition of a **majority holding** facilitates the consideration of other factors because of the greater freedom of action obtained by the investor (in terms of control of the organization thus acquired).

### The use of charts

Certain analysts argue that the use of charts, showing **trends in share prices** for past periods, can be extremely beneficial. Such analysts, known as chartists, argue that share prices follow certain well-defined patterns, and that critical decision points can be isolated by graphing the patterns for particular securities. Many other analysts are critical of this viewpoint, but it must be recognized that some use *is* undoubtedly made of charts. This is important in that if sufficient investors believe that a particular event will occur it may well actually happen. For example, if a large number of people believe that the shares of Smith Co. will rise to a price of $4 each, they will buy them at prices below $4, thus causing that price to be achieved. A similar logic applies to the use of charts.

## BUSINESS VALUATIONS

The valuation of a business is, in concept, no different to the valuation of a share or shares. However, a number of **other factors** are worthy of consideration.

**1.** Estimated cash inflows will generally relate to earnings rather than dividends. Where appropriate, **opportunity costs** should be included (e.g., salaries drawn by an owner for work done in the business), so as to ensure that a correct figure is obtained for returns *from the amount invested*.

**2.** Knowledge of **asset values** can be useful. **Replacement costs (RC)** enable a potential investor to ascertain how much it would cost to acquire the physical assets necessary to start such a business from scratch. **Net realizable values (NRV)** provide an indication as to the **bail-out facility** should the project go wrong. There is no logical financial reason for a business to be sold at a figure which is lower than the total of the NRVs of assets, less any external debts.

**3.** In acquiring a business as a going concern, some consideration needs to be given to the fact that acquisition brings with it certain advantages which would not be available to a new business, e.g., reputation, clientele, experienced work force, etc. These advantages are generally referred to as **goodwill**, and must be paid for. In certain industries conventions exist with regard to the amount paid for goodwill, but in the final analysis the amount is the result of negotiation by the parties to the agreement.

## RISK AND SECURITY VALUATION

In the context of security valuation, risk may be considered to be the extent to which the actual returns from a security could vary from those expected. This can be sub-divided into two aspects.

**1. Specific risk** is that part of the total risk which arises from features of the organization itself, and from features of the industry within which it operates.

**2. Systematic risk** is that part of the total risk which arises from features of the economy as a whole.

The difference between these two is extremely important, since specific risk can be eliminated by any particular shareholder merely by holding a portfolio of securities of different organizations from different industries. By contrast, systematic risk cannot be eliminated or even reduced by holding portfolios of shares. The relationship between total risk and the number of securities in a portfolio is shown in Figure 7.

Figure 7 clearly shows that much of the total risk attaching to any individual organization can be eliminated by holding a portfolio of securities. This explains why investors typically hold securities in portfolios. Figure 7 also shows that most of the specific risk can be eliminated by holding a portfolio of as little as ten securities. It further indicates that, irrespective of how many securities are held, there remains part of the total risk – the systematic risk – which the investor is forced to bear.

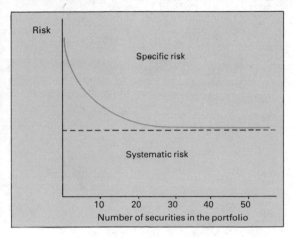

*Figure 7. Total risk and portfolio size*

Most **specific risk** can be eliminated easily and cheaply, investors cannot expect to obtain large returns to compensate them for bearing the risk. However, they can and do require compensation in the form of larger returns for bearing **systematic risk**.

Systematic risk is measured by a factor known as a **beta coefficient**. It measures the degree of correlation between the returns for an individual security and those of the market generally. Theoretically, the higher the coefficient, the higher the risk premium associated with the security. A security with a beta coefficient of zero should have *no risk premium*. Securities with negative coefficients should have *negative risk premiums*, i.e., their price is likely to be "bid up" because of their attractiveness as part of a portfolio, thus reducing the returns obtainable. In practice, securities with negative or zero beta coefficients are less common than those with positive betas.

## SHARE VALUATIONS AND EFFICIENT CAPITAL MARKETS

While certain doubts exist with regard to the applicability of some of the particular techniques or models discussed above, there appears to be a general acceptance that the market (i.e., the Stock Exchange) is, overall, fairly efficient. In other words, the prices obtaining at any moment in time reflect a balance of all the views in the market. If such a view is accepted, the question must be asked as to whether it is worth while spending time and effort in trying to value quoted securities. It would appear that share valuation is only worth undertaking where unquoted securities are involved or if efficiency is doubted. It is something of a paradox that efficiency only exists as long as people continue to try to "beat" the market.

# Chapter 8

# Take-overs and Mergers

## REASONS FOR TAKE-OVERS AND MERGERS

A business organization, as has already been stated, is concerned with making investments which will help it to achieve its corporate objectives. One way of doing this is to acquire assets currently managed by another organization, by acquiring ownership or control of this organization.

The main objective of the acquiring organization is likely to be to improve its own financial standing, obtained through an increase in its stock price. Thus, an organization might be viewed as a worthy **target** by an acquiring organization if the present value of benefits from acquisition exceed the present value of the costs of acquisition. Bearing in mind that present value has two components, cash flows and discount rate, an acquiring firm is likely to be attracted to a take-over if acquisition of the target firm will increase net present value by either of the following means.

**1.** Increasing the positive cash flows.
**2.** Reducing the level of risk of the cash flows and hence the discount rate.

Both factors may be involved in any particular take-over.

**Risk reduction** may be achieved in one or both of two ways.

**1.** Reduction of the risk in **running the original business** of the acquirer can be achieved, e.g., by taking over an organization which acts as a *major supplier* to the acquirer. By gaining control of the supplier, the acquirer is able to ensure that it always gets favorable treatment from that supplier. Similarly, obtaining control of a *major sales outlet* could ensure favorable treatment on the sales side.

**2.** Reduction in specific risk may be achieved by acquiring an organization whose **activities are dissimilar** from those of the acquirer. This is based on the approach of "not putting all of one's eggs in one basket". For example, if the acquirer's main activity is operating merchant ships, the acquisition of an organization whose main activity is newspaper publishing is likely to reduce risk. This is because recessions in merchant shipping are unlikely to coincide with those in newspaper publishing, thus keeping overall cash flows at a much more steady level than would be obtained from merchant shipping profits alone.

The take-over of existing organizations is by no means the only way of achieving risk reduction, but it can be a quick and effective means of achieving a major diversification.

Apart from risk reduction, a number of **other reasons for take-overs** exist, and the acquiring organization may well be influenced by the following aspects.

**1.** The level of management talent, expertise and experience in the target.

**2.** The market share of the target.

**3.** Particular physical assets (including cash) of the target.

**4.** Access to some technological advantage of the target.

**5.** The extent to which the two businesses would complement each other, such that the total could be greater than the sum of the parts (usually referred as a "synergy").

**6.** The greater access to finance (and other factors) open to larger organizations.

**7.** Potential benefits from the economies of scale which a larger operation may give rise to.

Take-over attempts frequently receive the blessing of the management of the target organization, and encouragement to the target's shareholders to sell their shares may well come from both sets of management. Whether a particular arrangement is considered a "merger" or a "take-over" is a question of semantics. The word **merger** is usually applied to situations where the organizations concerned are of a similar size, or where there is a measure of agreement between the two managements as to the desirability of an amalgamation. A **take-over** implies a difference in scale of the two organizations, or perhaps some lack of agreement between the managements on the desirability of the scheme.

## MEANS OF EFFECTING A TAKE-OVER

A take-over is typically achieved by one organization (the acquirer) buying sufficient **voting stock** in another organization (the target) so as to gain control of the latter. This may be effected by buying shares in the stock market or making a direct offer to each individual shareholder of the target for the sale of his shares. A particular take-over attempt may involve both of these approaches. In the initial stage of a take-over attempt the acquiring organization often buys shares in the target organization in the open market, obviously settling in cash.

When, as is typically the case, a **formal offer** is made to each of the remaining shareholders of the target organization, the offer will usually consist of one or more of the following.

**1.** Cash.
**2.** Shares (to be issued) of the acquirer.
**3.** Debt securities (to be issued) of the acquirer.

A shareholder in the target who accepts the offer will cease being a shareholder in that organization. If the offer is for cash, the shareholders of the target will have no affiliation with the merged firm. If the offer is for stock or debt securities the shareholder of the target will become a stock and/or a debt holder in the now enlarged acquiring organization. The acquirer will take his place as a shareholder in the target organization.

It should be noted that the issuing of stock or debt securities by an organization, to effect a take-over, is not an exercise which is undertaken without some cost. Stock or debt securities which are issued in exchange for shares in the target are obviously not being issued for cash, and an opportunity cost clearly exists.

## APPRAISAL BY THE ACQUIRING ORGANIZATION

Take-overs are, from the acquiring organization's viewpoint, simply an investment, and should be assessed as such. All cash flows expected to arise from the arrangement must be taken into account. These include the opportunity cost of any stock or debt securities issued, all future cash flows from business operations associated with the target, and any increases in overall cash flows resulting from the take-over (i.e., increases due to synergy). These cash flows must be discounted at a cost of capital appropriate to the level of risk involved with the particular activities concerned, in order to arrive at a figure for net present value. If the shareholders of the acquirer are to benefit from the take-over, this net present value must be positive. The **upper limit on the offer price**, therefore, should be one which will show a zero net present value when used in the above appraisal.

The management of the acquiring organization is likely to be seeking to maximize the benefit to its own shareholders, and so will try to **obtain control** or complete ownership of the target **for the minimum cost** to itself.

The exact nature of the offer made – shares, debt securities or cash – will be dictated by considerations such as the availability of cash and the likely reaction of the shareholders of the target organization to the offer. There is no magic about the make-up of the offer or its value. The entire process is an open market operation where one party seeks to buy some assets from a group who will only accept an offer which seems advantageous to them.

## APPRAISAL OF THE OFFER BY SHAREHOLDERS OF THE TARGET ORGANIZATION

The offer is as much an investment opportunity from the point of view of the shareholders of the target organization as from that of the acquiring organization. Such shareholders, therefore, should compare the likely future cash flows from holding their original investment with those which will arise by accepting the offer, both discounted at an appropriate rate. Of course, if these shareholders see **real possibilities of an increased offer**, they may well refuse the original offer even though it would otherwise have been acceptable from a net present value point of view.

It is not uncommon for targets in take-overs to be organizations which have been poorly or over-cautiously managed, leading to a low stock price. In such cases an acquiring organization may well see the possibility of major improvements in profits in the future, so that an offer worth much more than the current share price can be made. This relatively large offer price may well be sufficient to induce most of the shareholders of the target to sell, and yet still represent an advantageous deal from the acquirer's viewpoint.

## LEGAL ASPECTS OF MERGERS

A number of federal laws, and possibly state laws, must be considered in evaluating a merger. The basic concern of these laws is to restrict mergers that result in a company gaining monopoly power in its markets, or to restrict mergers that are not in the best interest of the acquired company's shareholders.

The first government attempt to control mergers that would result in a monopoly was the **Sherman Antitrust Act of 1890**, which made it illegal for firms to merge in order to restrain trade or attempt to monopolize commerce. The **Federal Trade Commission Act of 1914** extended the Sherman Act to include unfair or deceptive methods of competition. **The Clayton Act of 1914** reduced the level of proof required for the Sherman act to bar mergers that "tend" to create a monopoly. The Clayton Act has been interpreted to apply at a regional level of competition.

**The Williams Act of 1968** restricts the actions of acquiring companies. When more than 5% of a company's outstanding stock is acquired, the acquirer must inform the **Securities Exchange Commission** of his purpose for buying the stock. This act also specifies that if a firm makes a public offer for the shares of another company, the offer must remain outstanding for a specified period of time. This is intended to give the shareholders of the target company time to evaluate the offer and time for other companies to make a counter offer for the stock, thus increasing the level of competition in the market for take-overs.

## TAX CONSEQUENCES OF MERGERS

There are two types of tax treatments for mergers. In a **taxable merger** the selling shareholders recognize the capital gain from the sale of their stock. The acquiring company revalues the acquired firm's assets and uses the new values for depreciation. Thus the acquired firm's shareholders pay taxes while the acquiring company increases its depreciation tax shield by revaluing the assets. This tax treatment applies to mergers where the acquired firm's shareholder's do not maintain a significant continuing interest in the merged firm, e.g., an acquisition paid for with cash.

**A tax-free merger** results when the acquired firm's shareholders maintain a significant continuing interest in the merged firm, e.g., an acquisition paid for with the acquiring firm's stock. In this case, no taxes are due from the selling shareholder and the acquiring company cannot revalue the assets.

## TYPICAL TACTICS OF THE ACQUIRER AND TARGET ORGANIZATIONS

Where the proposed course of action is agreed between the managements of the two organizations, a joint statement will usually be sent to all shareholders of the target. This would typically advise them to accept the offer, giving reasons why it would be to their advantage to do so. The weight of the target board recommendation is usually sufficient to ensure the success of the proposed action.

Where the proposed course of action does *not* meet with the approval of the management of the target, it will take steps to **defend the existing position**. The type of steps which might be taken are outlined below.

**1.** Circulars may be sent to the shareholders, generally arguing against acceptance, and perhaps claiming that:

(a) the prospects of the target are better if it is not taken over;
(b) the proposed merger lacks commercial logic;
(c) the acquirer's offer is unrealistically low.

**2.** The target organization may release private information in an attempt to enhance the quoted share price and so discourage the shareholders from accepting the acquirer's offer.

**3.** The target organization may try to find a "friendly" acquirer or "white knight".

The acquirer will tend to support its original offer by countering the claims made by the board of the target. **Increasing the offer** in the face of resistance to acceptance by the shareholders is a typical ploy. In many cases there seems to be a deliberate policy to pitch the original offer price at a fairly low level, to enable the acquirer to score a psychological point by subsequently increasing the offer price.

Where defensive measures are taken by the target, the ensuing battle is often fought out with some bitterness.

## THE SUCCESS OF TAKE-OVERS AND MERGERS

Researchers who have studied behavior of stock prices during take-overs and mergers have published conflicting results. Some find that the shareholders in the acquiring firms gain as a result of mergers, others do not find any gain for the acquiring firm. All find that shareholders of the acquired company gain as a result of mergers. This is expected since a company could not be acquired for less than its market value. Other researchers have found that mergers tend to occur when stock prices are high. If the target's shareholders gain and the acquirer's shareholders don't lose, there is some economic benefit to mergers. However, given the limited gains to the acquirer, it is hard to explain the level of merger activity.

Other research suggests that take-overs and mergers rarely live up to the claims made for them in advance, and that there are usually few benefits to the acquirer from a commercial point of view (e.g., increased earnings). Many take-overs have been seen to be rather unhappy affairs, commercially. Possible **problems** include the following:

**1.** Difficulties may arise in managing the larger, and perhaps more diverse, operation.

**2.** Rivalries may develop between the two sets of management involved, with too much time and energy being expended by individual managers in establishing their place in the new hierarchy, thus reducing their contribution to the actual management of the organization.

**3.** There is a danger that after the take-over or merger has taken place, management may relax, almost expecting the new set-up to run itself. This danger is more likely where there has been a long and bitter battle between the two sets of management immediately prior to the merger.

The above results suggest an apparent paradox: mergers may not increase the wealth of the acquiring firm's shareholders and introduce little or no commercial benefit to the constituent organizations. Yet firms still enter into mergers and compete with each other in takeovers. There are several possible **explanations** of this.

**1.** The level of publicity typically associated with take-overs and mergers may alert the investing public to an investment possibility that it had previously overlooked, thus tending to increase share prices.

**2.** Gains to the acquiring firm are reflected in the stock price when the firm begins its acquisition program, not at the time of a particular acquisition.

**3.** Any reduction in risk attaching to the merged operation, as compared with that of the constituent organizations, should mean that investors would accept lower returns from it. This acceptance of lower returns is likely to lead to a higher share price.

**4.** Information coming to light during a bid period may leave investors with more certainty about the organizations, again causing a lowering of required returns.

**5.** The lack of commercial success may take some time to manifest itself, so that the effect on share prices is slow to emerge. In other words, the immediate benefits to share-holders may be relatively short-lived, gradually disappearing as time elapses.

**6.** Managers of acquiring firms may enter mergers to reduce the risk they face as managers, not to increase the wealth of their firm's shareholders.

# Chapter 9

# Management of Working Capital

As noted earlier, business organizations make investments that enable them to achieve their corporate objectives. A typical business will require investments in land, buildings, plant, machinery, inventory, accounts receivable (i.e., credit extended to customers) and cash. When organizations are assessing investment projects they must include the effects of investments in both durable goods such as plant and equipment and short-term (current) assets such as inventory and accounts receivable. The **current assets** are not a permanent part of the firm, they are systematically dissipated and then replaced as a normal part of the firm's operations.

As an **example** of how this dissipation and replacement occurs in practice, consider an organization which is engaged in wholesaling. The organization buys inventories of goods for resale. These goods are subsequently sold to customers on credit, and after a further lapse of time the customer will pay cash to settle his debt. Normally, the organization will wish to continue doing business and so it must replace the goods sold from inventory. As one customer pays his debt another customer is buying goods on credit, and as the cash for these goods is received by the organization it will have to be paid out to replace the goods sold from inventory. This transformation of inventory into accounts receivable, accounts receivable into cash and cash back into more inventory occurs in most business organizations.

Inventories, accounts receivable and cash tie up investment funds and also have other costly disadvantages. For this reason, organizations should always seek to **minimize the levels of these assets** and, ideally, reduce them to zero. As will be seen, however, reducing them to zero is rarely a practical proposition since to do so would result in a much greater risk of other adverse costs being incurred. The determination of the optimal levels for such assets is therefore the result of a **balancing process** between the costs of holding such assets and the risks associated with not holding them, or of holding only small amounts.

The importance of working capital management becomes much clearer if one considers the **statistical evidence**. Statistics for the United States indicate that commercial organizations invest as much in current assets as in fixed assets. Clearly, therefore, any steps which can be taken to minimize levels of current assets will probably yield large savings in costs.

The remainder of this chapter will examine working capital management in the following areas.

1. **Inventory.**
2. **Accounts receivable.**
3. **Cash.**

## MANAGEMENT OF INVENTORIES

For commercial organizations, inventories fall into three broad categories.

**1. Raw materials**–the various items which a manufacturing organization holds ready for use in the production process, as and when required.

**2. Work in progress**–the partially manufactured products of the manufacturing organization. It is likely to include products in varying stages of completion.

**3. Finished inventories**–inventories which are ready for sale by the organization. For a manufacturing organization these would be the finished product. For a retailing organization they would be stocks which have been bought in for resale.

As implied in the previous section, the management of inventory requires the identification and balancing of two kinds of costs.

**1.** Costs of holding inventories. These are the tangible costs which *increase* as the level of inventory increases.

**2.** Costs associated with holding zero or low levels of inventory. Such inventory levels carry with them certain types of risk, which could be substantially eliminated by holding larger amounts of inventory. These costs tend to *reduce* as the level of inventory increases.

### Costs of holding inventories
These costs tend to be fairly easily identifiable and include the following:

**1. Financing costs** These are the costs of providing funds to acquire the inventory held by the firm, i.e., the value at the inventory held multiplied by the cost of capital.

**2. Storage costs** These are the costs of physically accommodating the inventory. This would include such items as the rent of the storage space and the salaries of personnel employed in inventory supervision and control. In the case of perishable inventories, e.g., food, storage costs may well include such items as the cost of refrigeration, etc.

**3. Insurance cost** This is the cost of insuring the inventory against loss from theft, damage, etc. For particularly valuable inventories, security guards may also have to be employed.

**4. Cost of losses actually incurred** through theft, damage, etc., if not covered by insurance.

**5. Obsolescence cost** If inventories held go out of fashion, or design specifications change, these inventories may lose value. The longer inventories are held, the greater are the risks involved.

These costs can be considerable, and have been estimated to range from 20% to 100% per annum of the value of the inventory concerned. Exactly where in this range the annual inventory holding cost falls will depend on the type of inventory concerned. For example, a perishable good which is particularly susceptible to theft is likely to be towards the top of this range, whereas non-perishable goods such as builders' sand would be nearer the lower end.

### Costs of holding low (or zero) inventories
These costs tend to be rather less obvious, and the identification of actual amounts involved is difficult. Such costs include the following:

**1. Cost of loss of customer goodwill** If an organization is unable to supply its customers as and when they require supplies, it is likely to experience a loss of customer goodwill, with a subsequent damaging effect upon sales. The lower the inventory level held, the higher the probability of such costs being incurred. The extent to which a loss of goodwill actually occurs is likely to depend upon the market status of the organization. For example, a monopoly supplier may not suffer any effective loss of goodwill as a result of keeping customers waiting.

**2. Cost of production dislocation** This applies to raw material inventories and work in progress. Insufficient inventories may well result in production being held up. This in turn may mean that labor and other resources will become idle, even though costs continue to be incurred.

**3. Ordering costs** This relates to the cost of placing each order with a supplier, and includes associated costs such as handling the goods when delivered. The higher the number of orders, the greater the costs will be. Since low inventory levels will probably be associated with frequent replacement ordering, they are likely to be associated with higher ordering costs than high inventory levels. Another important factor is that orders for large quantities are frequently associated with **bulk discounts**, allowing further savings.

### Optimal inventory levels
In spite of the considerable difficulties involved in calculating the various costs referred to above, the organization should seek the balance that achieves the minimum total cost. In other words, it should determine the inventory level at which **total inventory costs are at a minimum**. The logic of this process can be seen from Figure 8, on the following page.

As the inventory level rises, so does the total of the costs of holding inventories. On the other hand, the costs associated with holding zero or low levels of inventory will fall as inventory levels increase. The total cost of holding inventory is the sum of these two types. The organization should seek to hold a level of inventory at which the total cost is at a minimum, i.e., point M on the diagram.

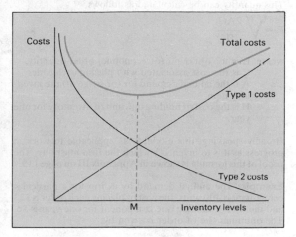

*Figure 8. Optimal inventory levels*

One **problem** with deciding the **optimal inventory level** is that unless inventory is replaced immediately when it is used, it will not be possible to maintain the exact inventory level desired. In practice, it is more likely that inventory will be used at a steady rate throughout the year, but replaced in large "blocks". The inventory level for a particular item over time is show in Fig. 9. In this case, the inventory level steadily falls to zero and is immediately replaced by a further amount of inventory (E). The new inventory level, in turn, steadily drops to zero, only to be replaced again. The actual inventory level is consequently always oscillating around the optimum inventory level (M).

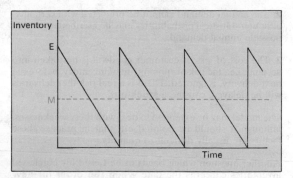

*Figure 9. Average inventory levels*

Once this process is recognized, another interesting question arises—what is the quantity of inventory (E) which should be bought in order to minimize costs? In other words, what is the **economic order quantity**?

This quantity can be calculated as follows.

$$E = \sqrt{\frac{2AC}{H}}$$

where E is the optimum (or economic) order quantity,
  C is the cost associated with placing each order,
  A is the annual demand for (or usage of) the inventory item,
  H is the cost of holding one unit of inventory for one year.

Broadly speaking, this model is as applicable to work in progress as it is to inventory which the firm must buy. The proof of this formula is shown in Appendix III on page 119.

**Example:** The annual demand by a firm for a particular component is 400 units, the cost of placing each order is \$23 and the cost of holding one component for one year is \$6. The optimum size of order is given by:

$$E = \sqrt{\frac{2 \times 400 \times 23}{6}} = 55.4$$

This means that the firm should place orders for 55 or 56 units of the component, thereby holding an average inventory of about 28 units.

The model above—for establishing order sizes—is widely used in practice, although it has the following easily identifiable **weaknesses**.

**1.** Demand for the inventory may fluctuate on a seasonal basis.

**2.** The annual demand cannot be predicted with certainty, although statistical probabilities may be ascribed to various possible annual demands.

**3.** The cost of loss of customer goodwill is not taken into account, i.e., the risk of running out of inventory, before the next delivery, is ignored. There is a real risk that deliveries will be delayed, causing a **stock-out**.

The model may be extended to deal with these weaknesses, although it should be pointed out that in practice these factors are usually difficult to quantify.

Another question which needs to be raised for purchased inventories concerns the date **when the order for new inventory should be placed**. The firm will know from experience how much time usually elapses between placing the order with the supplier and physical delivery of the good. This is usually referred to as the **lead-time**. The order should be placed such that the usage during the lead-time will reduce the inventory to zero by the time delivery occurs.

In the above example, the annual demand was 400 units or about 33 each month. If the lead-time is about 1.5 months, then the order should be placed when there are about 50 units (1.5 × 33) left in stock. Most organizations will build a **margin of safety** into the **re-order level** and, as in the above example, set the re-order level at some figure above 50 units. How much above 50 units would depend on management's assessment of the risk of either demand being greater than expected during the lead-time or the supplier taking longer than expected to deliver. In both cases there would be the danger of dislocation of production or loss of customer goodwill.

It must be recognized that the above model, while widely used, may not be sufficiently sophisticated for some organizations and many organizations will need to devise more complicated methods of analysis. All organizations ought to calculate their optimum order quantity and establish re-order levels incorporating a margin of safety. This exercise should be carried out for every individual inventory item and, once established, systematically applied in the day-to-day management of inventories.

## MANAGEMENT OF ACCOUNTS RECEIVABLE

With the exception of most types of retailing, commercial sales are usually made on credit. This means that **cash settlement lags some time behind the delivery** of the good or rendering of the service to which the payment relates. The main **reasons** for this practice are attributable to commercial convenience and, to some extent, commercial tradition. It is seldom convenient for cash to be collected at the same time that goods are delivered for the following reasons.

**1.** The recipient will need to assure himself that the goods are satisfactory prior to payment.

**2.** It is usually more convenient to use financial intermediaries, e.g., banks, to exchange large sums rather than transferring cash. This introduces a delay in the payment for the goods.

Even where it would be reasonably practical to pay on delivery, customers are reluctant to forgo the traditional credit period since to do so would increase their own financing costs. The practice of allowing credit has thus come to be widely accepted as normal. The use of credit has certain costs associated with it, and the management of accounts receivable requires a clear identification and balancing of various costs.

**1.** Costs of allowing credit.
**2.** Costs of refusing credit.

## Costs of allowing credit

Certain costs will *increase* as the amount of credit (and thus the level of accounts receivable) increases. Such costs include the following.

**1. Financing costs** These comprise the average amount due from customers multiplied by the organization's cost of capital.

**2. Costs of maintaining the necessary accounting records** It is necessary to keep a record for each customer showing how much is owed and for how long it has been owed.

**3. Costs of collecting the debts** Frequently customers need to be reminded that cash is due to be paid. Even if only one letter or telephone call results in payment, that communication costs money. Customers who, for some reason or another, show great reluctance to pay may be subject to legal action to effect recovery of the debt. However, this kind of back-up is expensive.

**4. Bad debts** If a customer cannot be made to pay, then the supplier not only loses his profit on the sale but has to bear the costs of the goods or service provided.

**5. Insurance cost** Bad debts may be insured against, at a cost.

**6. Cost of obtaining a credit reference** It is usual when first granting credit to a new customer to take up references, usually from an agency which specializes in credit references.

**7. Discounts** As an inducement for customers to pay promptly, organizations often offer their customers the right to deduct a small percentage (e.g., 2%) if they pay within a specified time from the date of the sale (e.g., 10 days).

**8. Inflation cost** Debts which are outstanding during a period of inflation will lose value in terms of purchasing power since the amount subsequently paid will be worth less than it was when the debt was incurred.

## Costs of refusing credit

These costs are more difficult to quantify, but include the following:

**1. Loss of customer goodwill** Since most organizations *do* allow their customers credit, a firm which refuses to allow credit would be at a considerable disadvantage when compared with its competitors which allow credit, causing a probable loss of trade. Such an organization can only compensate by offering some other inducement to its customers, for example lower prices than its competitors, although actions of this type do have their own associated costs.

**2. Inconvenience** An insistence on payment at the time of the rendering of the goods or service may well lead to an increase in security risk, since cash will be collected by a large number of individual employees, rather than being received at a central place.

### The optimal level of accounts receivable
As with the management of inventories, management should balance the two types of costs given above against each other in order to achieve a position of minimum total cost. This is not an easy task and there are no simple mathematical models to offer guidance in this matter.

However, assuming that an organization does not go to the extreme of refusing to allow credit, there are several **general rules** which should be followed.

**1.** Management should decide on its **general policy** towards allowing credit.

**2.** All new customers should be assessed for the **level of credit which should be allowed** them. Requiring references to be produced can be particularly useful in this respect.

**3.** The established credit levels should be **rigidly adhered to** unless a fundamental reappraisal of each customer's credit rating is undertaken.

**4.** Customers' accounts should be **constantly reviewed** and overdue customers reminded that payment is due.

Generally, the management of accounts receivable should be conducted in a systematic manner, in accordance with the policy on which management has decided and after taking all the relevant factors into account.

## MANAGEMENT OF CASH

Organizations need to hold a certain amount of cash for several reasons.

**1. Planned payments** for goods, services and wages, etc., need to be made.

**2.** A fund, as protection against **unexpected demands**, needs to be provided.

**3.** The organization needs to be able to take advantage of such **unexpected opportunities** as may arise.

As is the case with stocks and accounts receivable, cash has its own associated costs.

**1.** The costs of holding cash.

**2.** The costs of holding no cash (or low levels of cash).

**Costs of holding cash**
These fall into two main areas.

**1. Loss of interest** or other return which could be earned if the cash is invested in some way.
**2. Loss of purchasing power** if the cash is held during a period of inflation.

**Costs of holding no cash**
These costs tend to be less obvious and rather more difficult to quantify.

**1. The inability to meet bills as they occur** This will probably result in a loss of goodwill among suppliers and employees, and may well render the organization unable to continue in business. At best, this situation will lead to suppliers and employees requiring greater rewards as compensation for the uncertainty of the timing of their receipts.

**2.** The **opportunity cost** involved here is one of being unable to take up any unexpected opportunities which may arise (e.g., buying some cheap inventory item for cash).

**3.** There is a **cost associated with having to borrow** cash at expensive short-term rates to meet unexpected demands.

Once again, it is the responsibility of management to **balance these costs** with each other and so arrive at the optimal level of cash to be held.

One technique which offers particular assistance to cash management is that of **cash budgeting**. This is usually done for one year ahead, on a monthly basis. The cash inflows and outflows planned for each month are identified and the likely cash balances estimated from them. Steps can then be taken at an *early* stage in the planning process to remedy any cash shortfalls or to utilize cash surpluses. Cash budgets are frequently set out as follows.

| Cash inflows | January ($) | February ($) | March ($) |
|---|---|---|---|
| Debtors | 10300 | 11700 | 10100 |
| Cash sales | 2500 | 2500 | 2500 |
| Total inflows (A) | 12800 | 14200 | 12600 |
| | | | |
| **Cash outflows** | | | |
| Creditors | 7100 | 9200 | 10800 |
| Wages | 4600 | 4800 | 4800 |
| Total outflows (B) | 11700 | 14000 | 15600 |
| | | | |
| Surplus/(deficit) (A−B) | 1100 | 200 | (3000) |
| Cumulative surplus/(deficit) | 1100 | 1300 | (1700) |

In this example, it can be seen that cash surpluses are expected in January and February whereas in March a deficit is expected. If there were no cash in the bank on 1 January, the bank balance at the end of each month would be given by the cumulative surplus/(deficit) figure above. Using this budget, management must decide how it is going to overcome the deficit in March, and indeed how, if at all, it is going to use the cash surpluses of January and February. Of course, the cash flows shown in any budget are only estimates and so some margin of error should be incorporated. For example, in March the organization may well seek to have, say, $2000 available, giving a margin of $300.

In general terms, management should seek to look ahead and plan its cash requirements by using some form of cash budget. Leaving cash management to chance is likely to prove expensive and possibly fatal.

# Chapter 10

# Cost of Capital and Choice of Discount Rate

## THE CONCEPT

The theoretical decision rule for a firm's capital investment was developed in Chapter 6. This rule is to accept those projects whose return exceeds a specified discount rate. We now discuss how to determine that rate.

In principle it can be said that **the discount rate should be based upon the cost of funds** if the overall aim is, as is generally assumed, the *maximization of shareholders' wealth*. The net present value (NPV) of an organization will be increased with each new investment that yields a return greater than the cost of funds. From this it should be clear that to achieve maximum NPV, an organization should continue to invest in projects until the **expected returns on the marginal investment** equal the **marginal cost of funds** used, i.e., projects should be accepted where one of the following conditions holds true.

**1.** The NPV is positive when returns are discounted at the marginal cost of funds.

**2.** The yield from projects is greater than the marginal cost of funds.

As indicated in Chapter 1, organizations may have objectives that would use decision rules other than the maximization of shareholders' wealth. While there is little doubt that other objectives exist, maximization of shareholders' wealth appears to be more widely accepted than most other objectives. If such an objective *is* accepted or used to determine decision rules, the organization clearly **needs to know its marginal cost of funds**.

In a perfect world, where knowledge is based on certainty, all types of funds would have identical costs since no risk would exist, and the interest rate would entirely reflect an allowance for the time value of money. Hence, under conditions of certainty this interest rate would serve as the cost of capital and discount rate. However, in practice, a **range of costs** exists because funds can be raised from a variety of sources, each with different associated risks and therefore differing costs. For example, the use of debentures involves the payment of interest, which must occur irrespective of the level of profits, whereas dividends to ordinary shareholders are dependent on profits. Hence, the cost of debentures is likely to be lower than that of shares. Some loans are secured or have a prior claim on assets of the firm if the firm goes bankrupt. Such loans would normally be associated with lower interest rates than unsecured loans, which in turn would normally be associated with lower returns than those expected for ordinary shares. Given the situation in which a range of funds *is* used, the question must be asked as to the cost of funds to be used in investment decisions. In answering this question, the following points will be considered.

**1.** The cost of individual types of funds.

**2.** The concept of the weighted average cost of capital.

Before embarking on this answer, however, a number of **general points** need to be made.

**1.** The cost of funds should be seen as an *opportunity cost,* obtained from the market or imputed, e.g., retained earnings cannot be regarded as free since they impose opportunity costs on shareholders. If one particular source of funds is used, the cost of other funds may well change. Hence, market price and opportunity cost frequently differ.

**2.** The cost of funds must relate to the estimated cost of obtaining funds at the time at which they are actually required for the purchase of further products. They are, therefore, *expected* figures at the time a project is undertaken. Having said this, the calculation of the *current* cost of funds is generally considered to provide a fairly accurate figure, given the acknowledged efficiency of the market.

**3.** In arriving at the cost of individual sources of funds, a number of assumptions need to be made about valuation models for different securities. Modifications to these valuation models will clearly affect the cost of funds calculation.

**4.** The *cost of funds* is the amount which needs to be paid to a provider of funds for the use of those funds. It is equal to the returns required by the provider of funds. Hence, the calculation of currently obtainable returns from different types of securities gives a good guide to the cost of these new funds.

## COST OF EQUITY CAPITAL

Equity holders invest in shares in the expectation of obtaining returns in the form of dividends and/or capital gains. There are only two ways of providing further equity finance.

**1. New equity issues.**

**2. Retained earnings.**

### New Issues

A new issue of shares will normally be made only if the returns from this issue are such that share prices would increase. One would not expect an issue of shares to be made with the *expectation* that share prices would fall, since this would reduce shareholders' wealth. Hence, it can be said that the *minimum* return required from a new issue is that which would leave the share price at its present level.

In the absence of any issue costs, or changes in investors' attitudes towards the organization, this return would be the rate at which the market capitalizes future earnings—which in practice means the current return obtained from the existing shares.

It is apparent from the section in Chapter 7 on share valuations that **a number of valuation models** can be used. If the current market price is known, it is then quite easy to work out the return that is currently being achieved. For example, consider a **dividend valuation model**, such that:

$$P_0 = \sum_1^\infty \frac{D_n}{(1 + k)^n}$$

where $P_0$ = present share price,
    $D_n$ = dividends in year n,
    $k$ = required rate of return.

This model is concerned with calculating present share price by discounting future dividends at an appropriate rate. If current share price is known, and dividends can be estimated, k can then be calculated.

**Example:** The current market price of a share is $10 and annual dividends per share are expected to amount to $1.20 for an indefinite period in the future.

$$\$10 = \frac{\$1.20}{(1+k)} + \frac{\$1.20}{(1+k)^2} + \frac{\$1.20}{(1+k)^3} + \ldots + \frac{\$1.20}{(1+k)^n}$$

which reduces to    $\$10 = \dfrac{\$1.20}{k}$

therefore k    $= \dfrac{\$1.20}{\$10} = 0.12$ or 12%.

In other words, the market expects a 12% return from a share in this particular risk category.

Suppose now that this particular organization is 100% equity financed and has 10 000 shares. Assume also that the whole of its profits are distributed as dividends so that expected future dividends are $12 000 per annum. A new project costing $20 000 is being considered, which will give an increase in net annual earnings of $3000 for the foreseeable future all of which will be distributed. If the project were to be financed by a new issue of 2000 shares at a price of $10 per share, should it be accepted?

If the project is accepted the value of the organization, using the dividend valuation model, would be expected to become:

$$P_0 = \frac{\$15\,000}{(1+k)} + \frac{\$15\,000}{(1+k)^2} + \frac{\$15\,000}{(1+k)^3} + \ldots + \frac{\$15\,000}{(1+k)^n}$$

$$P_0 = \frac{\$15\,000}{0.12} = \$125\,000$$

Since 12 000 shares now exist, the market price per share would be expected to rise to $10.42. As shareholders' wealth has been increased the project should be accepted.

A moment's reflection should make it clear that as long as the return on the new project exceeds 12% the project should be accepted. At a 12% return on the new investment dividends would increase by $2400 to $14 400. The value of the company would thus become:

$$P_0 = \frac{\$14\,400}{(1+k)} + \frac{\$14\,400}{(1+k)^2} + \frac{\$14\,400}{(1+k)^3} + \ldots + \frac{\$14\,400}{(1+k)^n}$$

$$P_0 = \frac{\$14\,400}{0.12} = \$120\,000$$

Since there would now be 12 000 shares, market price per share would remain at $10.

If organizations are expected to grow in terms of earnings and dividends, the dividend valuation model ceases to be appropriate, and the use of **growth models** should be considered, e.g.,

$$P_0 = \frac{D_1}{k - g}$$

where  $P_0$ = present share price,
$D_1$ = dividends receivable one year from now,
$k$ = required rate of return,
$g$ = assumed growth rate in earnings and dividends.

If current share price is known, and acceptable estimates of future dividends and likely growth rates can be made, then the required rate of return can be derived.

**Example:** The current market price of a share is $10. Dividends per share are currently $.53, but earnings, dividends and market value are all expected to grow at a constant rate of 6% per annum.

$$P_0 = \frac{D_1}{k - g}$$

$$\$10 = \frac{\$0.53}{k - 0.06} \quad \text{therefore} \quad 10k - 0.60 = 0.53$$

$$k = \frac{0.53 + 0.60}{10} = 0.113 \text{ or } 11.3\%$$

This rate is the measure of the cost of equity capital for an organization with growth potential.

## Relaxation of assumptions

**1.** The examples have so far assumed that **no issue costs** are incurred. This situation is obviously not realistic, and adjustments would be needed in practice. It should be clear that *extra* returns would be needed to cover issue costs, so that the cost of new equity issues is likely to be slightly *higher* than was implied in the examples used above.

**2.** The second assumption, implicit in the above analysis, was that no changes would take place in investors' attitudes towards the organization as a result of changes in equity. In other words, it was assumed that investors would put an organization into the same **risk category** both before and after the change in equity. This assumption may not be valid, as additional projects may be considerably more risky, and investors may well add a larger risk premium to their required rate of return in order to compensate for additional risk. This can lead to extremely high marginal costs of equity and must be incorporated into the decision-making process. Alternatively, additional projects may actually reduce the perceived risk associated with the organization, thus giving lower marginal costs of equity.

**3.** In the above examples, it was assumed that expectations about dividends and growth would *all* be communicated to, and accepted by, the market, and reflected in prices. This is also unlikely to be true in practice, at least not with the degree of precision implied.

Relaxation of these assumptions poses practical problems for the calculation of the cost of equity capital, and results will not be as easily or as precisely obtained as was perhaps implied in the examples given earlier. Nevertheless, the earlier analysis provides a framework within which calculations can be made, with amendments being made as necessary to take account of the matters referred to in this section.

## Cost of retained earnings
Retained earnings are the single most important source of equity funds for business organizations, particularly for purposes of expansion and growth.

Retained earnings have no direct cost but have a clear **opportunity cost**. If profits are paid out as dividends, shareholders can invest part or all of these dividends to make further returns. If profits are retained, the opportunity for shareholders to obtain such additional returns is eliminated. These forgone opportunities will need to be made up by the organization in the form of future dividends or growth in share values. These internal returns should amount to at least as much as the returns potentially available from investment made outside the company in a project of the same risk category.

**Example:** Consider an organization with earnings of $12 000 and equity of 50 000 shares, with a current market value of $2 per share (total market value $100 000). In the past, all profits have been distributed as dividends, and the market expects earnings and dividends to remain constant over time.

From this it should be clear that the required rate of return is 12%. This represents an appropriate return to shareholders, given their expectations about dividends and their view of the risk category of the investment. It is likely to be a rate of return which is *generally achievable* in the market for organizations in the same risk category. There is thus no reason for an investor to accept *less* than a 12% return. If greater returns were available elsewhere, and for the same level of risk, one would expect shareholders to sell their shares and put their funds into this more profitable area. The 12% rate therefore represents an **equilibrium rate of return**.

Suppose that the organization is now considering cutting its dividend from $24 per share to $14 per share, thereby retaining $5000 for use on a new project which will increase future dividends indefinitely by $750 per annum. The present value of these extra dividends, when discounted at 12%, is $6250. Since the sacrifice made by shareholders is $5000 in dividends, the overall increase in NPV is $1250, so the share price should increase to reflect the increase in the NPV of the firm. If the increased dividends were only $600 per annum (i.e., a 12% return) no increase in NPV would result. If the increase in dividends in future years is less than 12%, shareholders' wealth–as measured by NPV–would decrease. Thus, the **same decision rule applies to retentions as to new issues**.

One significant problem with regard to the cost of retentions concerns **taxation**. Individuals with high marginal tax rates for dividend purposes may well prefer retentions, since capital gains are taxed at a lower rate. However, the tax position of stockholders is likely to vary considerably from one stockholder to another, so the derivation of an appropriate cost is somewhat complex. Where possible, management should attempt to balance out these conflicting interests. If this cannot be done, it is usual to use the cost of retained earnings as calculated above.

## COST OF DEBT

The cost of new debt can normally be ascertained by reference to the interest rate payable. If $1m of debentures are issued at par, with an interest rate of 10%, the before tax cost of that debt would be 10%, if transactions costs were ignored. If transactions (issue) costs are incurred, or debt is not issued at par, certain adjustments must be made.

**Example:** $1m of perpetual debt is issued at 98 (i.e., at a discount of 2%). Issue costs amount to $40 000. The nominal interest rate is 10%.

|                          | $                          |
| ------------------------ | -------------------------- |
| Net cash inflows         | 980 000 ($1m × 0.98)       |
| Less issue costs         | 40 000                     |
| Cash received by the firm | 940 000                   |
| Annual interest          | 100 000                    |

Therefore before tax cost of debt
$$= (\$100\,000/\$940\,000) \times 100\% = 10.64\%$$

Often, the cost of debt needs to be ascertained by reference to the *return actually required by existing lenders*. If the market is functioning correctly, the rate of return currently being achieved on existing debt should be the rate that would be required for a new issue of debt in the same risk category. Since the interest rate effectively required may well *now* be different to the rate specified in the loan agreement, the calculations become a little more complex.

**Example:** A perpetual bond with a par value of $100 and a coupon rate of interest of 5%, currently sells at $50. The current effective return on this security can be ascertained by solving the following equation.

$$P_0 = \frac{I}{k}$$

where $I$ = annual interest,
$P_0$ = current market price,
$k$ = return.

Therefore       $\$50 = \dfrac{\$5}{k}$

hence           $k = \dfrac{5}{50} = 0.10$ or 10%.

Where debt is redeemable – which is the more typical case – maturity values also need to be considered, and calculations made similar to those on page 71.

In general terms, one would expect to find that the cost of debt was *lower* than the cost of equity since interest payments are rather more certain. Interest payments are a contractual requirement and are normally made even in periods of losses. Also, in the event of a liquidation, lenders' claims are satisfied before those of shareholders.

One further factor which needs to be considered with regard

to the cost of debt is the **effect of taxation**. The lender will have to pay taxes to the Internal Revenue Service on the interest he receives. The actual return he receives is the interest payment less the taxes paid on the interest. Hence, as far as the borrowing organization is concerned, the *gross* interest rate represents the cost. However, interest on debt is a deductible expense for purposes of corporate taxation, so a saving in corporation tax should occur. This should therefore be considered in calculating the cost of debt.

**Example:** A company issues $1m of debentures with an interest rate of 10%. Corporation tax rate on profits is 50% and profits will be earned even after interest has been deducted.

The cost of debt is not the 10% implied by the interest rate. The $100 000 annual interest payments are deducted from the company's profits before taxes. Thus, the after tax profits are reduced by $50 000 due to the debt issue. The cost of debt to the corporation is 5%.

## COST OF PREFERRED SHARES

The cost of preferred shares can be calculated along broadly similar lines to those applying to the cost of debt except that, since preferred dividends are not an allowable expense for corporate tax purposes, the taxation adjustment is not appropriate. For this reason, and the fact that preferred shares are more risky than debt, the cost of preferred shares is likely to be higher than the cost of debt.

## THE EFFECT OF LEVERAGE ON THE COSTS OF CAPITAL

In considering the costs of individual sources of capital, the effect of leverage on those costs has so far been ignored. However, in practice, it is likely that increases in the proportion of debt in the capital structure will lead to increases in the required rate of return for both shareholders and lenders.

As far as **shareholders** are concerned, the use of debt has three **main effects**.

**1.** It increases the spread or variance of possible returns.

**2.** It changes the expected returns to shareholders.

**3.** It increases the risk of bankruptcy (complete loss) through liquidation.

**Example:** Two companies have identical operating costs and associated revenues, giving profits of $100 000 per annum before tax. (Assume the corporate tax rate is 50%.) One company is 100% equity financed. The other is 50% financed from debt, on which interest at 10% is to be paid, and 50% from equity. Total funds in both companies amount to $400 000. The returns to shareholders can be calculated as follows.

|                        | 100% equity | 50% debt |
|------------------------|-------------|----------|
| Profit                 | 100 000     | 100 000  |
| less interest          | –           | 20 000   |
|                        | 100 000     | 80 000   |
| less taxation          | 50 000      | 40 000   |
| Returns to shareholders | 50 000     | 40 000   |
| Equity                 | 400 000     | 200 000  |
| Return to shareholders | 12.5%       | 20%      |

If operating profits *increased* to $150 000 the figures would become:

|                        | 100% equity | 50% debt |
|------------------------|-------------|----------|
| Profit                 | 150 000     | 150 000  |
| less interest          | –           | 20 000   |
|                        | 150 000     | 130 000  |
| less taxation          | 75 000      | 65 000   |
| Returns to shareholders | 75 000     | 65 000   |
| Equity                 | 400 000     | 200 000  |
| Return to shareholders | 18.75%      | 32.5%    |

If operating profits *fell* to $20 000, the figures would become:

|                        | 100% equity | 50% debt |
|------------------------|-------------|----------|
| Profit                 | 20 000      | 20 000   |
| less interest          | –           | 20 000   |
|                        | 20 000      | 0        |
| less taxation          | 10 000      | –        |
| Returns to shareholders | 10 000     | –        |
| Equity                 | 400 000     | 200 000  |
| Return to shareholders | 2.5%        | 0        |

From this it should be clear that the spread of possible returns is *increased* considerably as the proportion of debt increases. Also, if expected profits were $100 000 per year before tax, the expected return to shareholders would be *higher* for businesses with 50% debt than for firms with 100% equity. In addition, operating profits need to be maintained at a minimum of $20 000 per effecdentyear for the business with 50% debt, if shareholders are to avoid default on the debt.

For all of these reasons *the cost of equity capital is likely to rise as the proportion of debt capital increases. Hence the real cost of debt is not the cost as previously calculated, since additional costs will be added to the cost of equity.*

As far as **lenders** are concerned, it is likely that increases in the proportion of debt will be perceived as increasing the risk involved, since the coverage for both interest and principal is likely to be reduced. This will almost certainly lead to **increases in the cost of debt as the proportion of debt in the capital structure increases**.

## AVERAGE COST OF CAPITAL

In practice, organizations do not usually relate specific methods of finance to individual projects. As was pointed out earlier, issues of debt may well increase the cost of equity, so the real cost of capital may differ from those stated for a particular security. It is *not* appropriate to use a discount rate which is equal to the specific cost of *one* particular source of capital to appraise projects. *In the long term,* projects will be financed by a mixture of debt and equity, and **the appropriate discount rate is thus the average cost of capital**.

It must be recognized that the weighted average cost of capital will only be appropriate *if* the firm continues to raise funds in exactly the same proportions and undertakes projects with the same risk as the firm. This would also only be optimal if the capital structure were itself at an optimal level. Once these assumptions are made clear, the **rationale for the use of a weighted average cost of capital** becomes more evident. For example, consider an organization with an optimal debt equity ratio of 50%, and which has a new project that requires additional funds of $100 000, yielding a return of 8%. It is highly unlikely that the additional funds needed will always be raised in *exactly* the proportions implied by the optimal capital structure ratio. Over a longer period of time such an objective can be more easily achieved. However, in the short term it is probable that variations from the optimal position will occur. Suppose that in the above example the entire $100 000 was raised in the form of a debenture issue at 6%. Since the project yields a return of 8%, it might be argued that the project should be accepted. Suppose that another project costing $100 000 was proposed one year later, this time yielding a return of 12% but to be funded by equity, to enable a move back towards the optimal capital structure. If the cost of equity were 14%, it might then be argued that the project should be rejected. Clearly, such an anomalous position cannot be maintained, and the **use of the average cost of capital** (in this case 10%) **provides a more appropriate long-term discount rate**. If an organization finances itself in the long run in the optimal proportions, and accepts only projects with a yield in excess of the average cost of capital, it will tend to increase its shareholders' wealth.

To illustrate this point, consider this rule in relation to the above example. The optimal capital structure is assumed to be made up of 50% debt and 50% equity, with the cost of debt being 6%, the cost of equity 14% and the weighted average cost of capital 10%. A new project costing $100 000 will increase profits indefinitely by $10 000 per annum, thus yielding a return of 10%. This $10 000 is sufficient to give lenders a return of 6% and shareholders a return of 14%, as shown in the middle column below.

| | | |
|---|---|---|
| Return | $10 000 | $13 000 |
| Interest on debt ($50 000 at 6%) | $3 000 | $3 000 |
| Shareholders' returns | $7 000 | $10 000 |
| As a percentage on the $50 000 invested | 14% | 20% |

If project returns exceed 10%, the return to shareholders will be greater than the cost of equity, and share prices would tend to increase. The return to the shareholders is 20%. This is above their required return of 14%.

When calculating the average cost of capital, **weights** must be used for equity and debt. Two possibilities exist – book value and market value. These values may well differ quite considerably, but there is little doubt that **market values** are the more appropriate.

**Example:** A company is financed by 500 000 ordinary shares and by 1 000 000 10% perpetual debentures with par value of $1 each. The current market price of each share is $3.00 and of each debenture $0.80. The ordinary shares are expected to pay a dividend of $0.30 in one year's time and future dividends are expected to increase steadily by 5% per year. What is the weighted average cost of capital? Assume corporation tax is 50%.

**Cost of equity**

If $P_0 = \dfrac{D_1}{K_e - g}$

then $K_e = \dfrac{D_1}{P_0} + g$

i.e. $K_e = \dfrac{0.30}{3.00} + 0.05 = 0.10 + 0.05 = 15\%$

**Cost of debt**

$K_d = \dfrac{I}{P_0}$ i.e., $K_d = \dfrac{0.10}{0.80} = 12.5\%$

This is equivalent to an after tax cost of 6.25%.

**Current market values**

| | $ |
|---|---|
| Equity (500 000 × $3.00) | 1 500 000 |
| Debt (1 000 000 × $0.80) | 800 000 |
| Total market valuation | 2 300 000 |

## Weighted average cost of capital (WACC)

$$\textbf{WACC} = \left(\frac{1\,500\,000}{2\,300\,000} \times 15\% \right) + \left(\frac{800\,000}{2\,300\,000} \times 12.5\% \right)$$

$$= \quad 9.78 + 4.35 = 14.13\%$$

# Chapter 11

# Cost of Capital and Capital Structure

In the previous chapter, individual costs of capital were discussed, and the weighted average cost of capital was established as the appropriate discount rate to be used, if the organization were to continue raising funds in the same proportions for projects of the same risk as the firm. This chapter deals with capital structure in more detail and, in particular, with the question of whether or not an optimal capital structure exists. It also deals with the closely related area of dividend policy. Two main schools of thought exist with regard to the area of **capital structure**.

1. The **traditional** view.
2. The **Modigliani–Miller** view.

The differences between the two schools of thought are mainly attributable to different views being taken in the area known as **financial risk**. This is concerned with the increase in risk borne by shareholders as the proportion of debt in the capital structure increases. As this proportion rises, the financial risk increases, and the cost of both debt and equity is likely to rise. However, the *exact* nature of these increases in costs is far from clear, and different assumptions about this effect can lead to rather different views on capital structure.

## TRADITIONAL VIEW

The traditional view of capital structure is that financial risk is not perceived as increasing significantly until a certain level of debt is reached. Beyond this point, however, increased returns are required by lenders to compensate for the perceived extra risk. Similarly, the cost of equity is not likely to rise as soon as debt is introduced, but will only do so after a certain level of debt is reached. If debt reaches very high proportions the cost of both equity and debt are expected to rise sharply, such that any advantages of debt are likely to be cancelled out. The costs of debt and equity are illustrated in Figure 10. If cost of equity ($k_e$) and cost of debt ($k_d$) are known at different levels of leverage, the average cost of capital (i.e., equivalent to the average required rate of return by providers of funds) at different levels of leverage can also be calculated as shown.

Given the assumptions of the traditional model, the average cost curve will be U-shaped (some might say saucer-shaped). This implies that at the leverage ratio designated by X, the market valuation of the company will be at a maximum since returns are discounted at the lowest rate. Since maximization of shareholder wealth is taken to be the organization's overall objective, X represents the optimal debt/equity ratio.

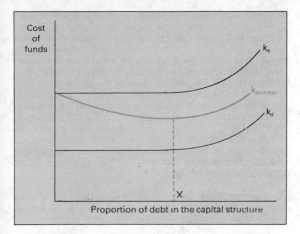

*Figure 10. Optimal capital structure–traditional view*

## THE MODIGLIANI–MILLER (MM) VIEW

Modigliani and Miller (1958) put forward a different view, arguing that the value of an organization should be independent of its financial structure *(if taxation is ignored)*. Value should be determined by the expected operating earnings, and two organizations in the same risk category and with equal operating earnings ought to be valued at the same price, irrespective of the level of debt. In other words, **total market value of an organization** (and therefore its cost of capital) **should be independent of the debt/equity relationship**.

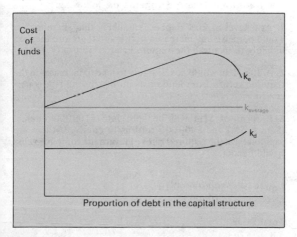

*Figure 11. Optimal capital structure–the Modigliani–Miller view*

The above argument is intuitively appealing. The total market value of an organization should not depend on its level of debt. This implies that weighted average cost of capital would need to stay constant over a range of debt/equity ratios. To see this, consider two identical firms that distribute all of their earnings to security holders. The total value of these firms is the present value of the payments to their security holders, using the weighted average cost of capital as the discount rate. Therefore, if the value of the firm does not change due to changes in capital structure, the weighted average cost of capital must be a constant. This implies that the cost of equity rises *as soon as* debt is issued and continues to rise as further debt is issued. Hence, the effective cost of debt equals the cost of equity. This position is shown diagrammatically in Figure 11.

At extreme levels of leverage, where the cost of debt increases, the MM view implies a reduction in the cost of equity. This point will be referred to again later.

## THE THEORIES CONTRASTED

The implications of the two schools of thought can be seen by considering a single company, with operating assets of $10m and operating earnings of $1m. Suppose that with 100% equity finance, the market values the company at $10m, indicating a cost of equity capital of 10% (and also a weighted average cost of capital of 10%).

If the capital structure was changed to 80% equity (e.g., 800 000 $1 shares) and 20% debt (e.g., 200 000 $1 5% debentures), what would happen to the cost of capital and total market value?

The **traditional theory suggests** the following:

**1.** At a level of 20% debt it is unlikely that shareholders would perceive any increases in risk and therefore they are unlikely to increase the required rate of return ($k_e$).

**2.** A 20% debt would not be likely to lead to increases in the required return from lenders as no increase in risk is perceived.

**3.** Returns of $1m will be split into $100 000 interest ($2m × 5%) and $900 000 returns to equity. If these are capitalized at the required rates of return the company value would become:

|        |                   | $m   |
|--------|-------------------|------|
| Equity | $900 000/0.10     | = 9  |
| Debt   | $100 000/0.05     | = 2  |
| Total value |              | 11   |

Hence, the traditional theory suggests that the **judicious**

**use of debt can increase the total company valuation**. This means that the weighted average cost of capital is given by

$1m/$11m × 100% = 9.09%.

Assume now that the level of debt is increased to 50% (i.e., $5m shares and $5m debentures). What does the traditional theory suggest for this?

**1.** At this level of debt the required rate of return is likely to increase substantially to, say, 8%.

**2.** The variance of returns to shareholders will increase and therefore the return required by shareholders is also likely to increase to, say, 15%.

**3.** Returns of $1m will be split into $400000 interest ($5m × 8%) and $600000 returns to equity. If these are capitalized at the above rates total valuation would become:

|  |  | $m |
|---|---|---|
| Equity | $600000/0.15 | 4 |
| Debt | $400000/0.08 | 5 |
| Total value |  | 9 |

Hence, the traditional theory suggests that **the use of debt beyond a certain point is likely to be counterproductive, and will lead to a reduced total valuation** because the perceived risk causes the cost of capital to rise. The weighted average cost of capital in the above case is given by

$1m/$9m × 100% = 11.1%.

Further increases in debt are likely to raise the cost of funds even more.

Using the **MM approach** the conclusions drawn are rather different. The essence of the MM argument is that total valuation ought to reflect total earning and should not be influenced by the capital structure. Hence, using the above example, the company should be capitalized at 10% throughout. If this is true, the cost of equity must increase as debt increases, although certain problems arise at high levels of debt. This can be seen below, where cost of equity is a residual calculation. The effect of different assumptions about the rate of interest on debt can also be seen.

|  | 100% equity | 20% debt | 50% debt | 50% debt |
|---|---|---|---|---|
| Cost of debt | – | 5% | 5% | 8% |
| Cost of equity | 10% | 11.25% | 15% | 12% |
| Weighted average | 10% | 10% | 10% | 10% |
| Market price per share | $1 | $1 | $1 | $1 |

This inevitably leads to the question as to *why* this degree of precision should exist in the market. Might not shareholders prefer the risk/return profile offered by a moderately levered organization? If they do, the position set out by the traditional theory would seem to be perfectly reasonable.

The essence of the MM argument is that it is not logical to expect a levered organization to sell at a higher price than an unlevered one. Investors can borrow money to buy stock creating **home-made leverage** (personal leverage). If an investor uses home-made leverage he obtains the same returns from an unlevered organization as from one which is levered, *without* any increase in financial risk. If this is so, no one should be prepared to pay more for a levered organization than for an unlevered one.

**Example:** By referring back to the previous example, the traditional theory suggests that shares should be valued as follows.

|                                  | $           |                              |
|----------------------------------|-------------|------------------------------|
| Levered company (assuming 20% debt) | 1.125 | (i.e. $900 000/800 000) |
| Unlevered company                | 1           |                              |

The shareholder in the levered company is incurring the financial risk associated with a 20% holding of debt. The shareholder in the unlevered company is not, and could borrow an equivalent amount without increasing his financial risk beyond that of the shareholder in the levered company. A shareholder with $90 000 to invest would be able to acquire 80 000 shares in a levered company which would give a return of $9000, or 10% on his investment.

Alternatively, the shareholder could acquire the same holding of equity in the unlevered company by putting up $64 000 of his own money and $16 000 of borrowed money. If the rate of interest payable on debt is the same for the individual shareholder as for the levered company (i.e., 5%), returns to the shareholder would be as follows.

| 80 000 shares at 10% return       | $8 000   |
| less interest ($16 000 × 5%)      | $800     |
|                                   | ———      |
| Net return                        | $7 200   |
| Net investment                    | $64 000  |
| Return as a percentage            | 11.25    |

In summary, the levered company was assumed to sell at a price of $1.125, and yielded a return of 10%. The unlevered company, which was assumed to sell at $1 per share, yielded 11.25% when home-made leverage was used to obtain equivalent financial risk. This situation cannot exist in equilibrium; investors would not be willing to pay $1.125 for a levered share of stock that offers a lower return as a stock that they can buy for $1 and lever themselves. This difference will be eliminated and the equilibrium price will be determined by **arbitrage**.

## ASSUMPTIONS OF THE MM ANALYSIS

It must be recognized that the above analysis is only valid if certain assumptions are made. Four assumptions are considered to be the most critical to the MM analysis.

**1.** A world of no taxes.
**2.** Rational economic behavior.
**3.** No transaction costs.
**4.** Individuals can borrow at the same rate of interest as commercial organizations.
**5.** Organizations in equivalent risk categories can be identified.

When **taxes** are introduced into the MM analysis the solution changes somewhat in that interest on debt is an expense for taxation purposes. This means that a levered firm should be able to distribute more to its shareholders and lenders than an unlevered firm.

**Example:** Assume a company with $10m in assets is financed in one of two ways.

**1.** 100% equity.
**2.** 80% equity, 20% debt (at 5%).

Operating earnings are $2m. All earnings are distributed as dividends. Distributable earnings under these two alternative capital structures are as follows.

|  | 100% equity ($m) | 80% equity ($m) |
|---|---|---|
| Operating earnings | 2 | 2 |
| less interest | – | 0.1 |
|  | 2 | 1.9 |
| less tax (assume 50%) | 1 | 0.95 |
| Dividends | 1 | 0.95 |
| Total distributed to shareholders and lenders | 1 | 1.05 |

This in turn means that the total value of the company should be higher for a levered company than for an unlevered one. Carried to its logical conclusion, this implies that an organization should use as much debt as possible in its capital structure. However, the use of extreme leverage poses other problems and it is unlikely to be a practical proposition for many firms.

Relaxation of the other three assumptions referred to above poses certain practical problems for the MM approach, and the general effect is to prevent the analysis being followed through with the precision implied in earlier sections. In particular, it is unlikely that an individual will be able to borrow either the same quantities or at the same cost as a commercial undertaking. In practice, "home-made" leverage is not a substitute for organizational leverage, so the arbitrage process is unlikely to work as precisely as implied above.

## CONCLUSIONS ON CAPITAL STRUCTURE

Both the traditional theory and the MM approach, *incorporating taxes,* suggest that total value of an organization will increase (or cost of capital will fall) as the level of debt is increased up to a certain point. Beyond this point, the theories conflict, with the traditional theory implying that total valuation will eventually fall as debt increases while the MM approach suggests that it will continue to rise as debt increases. The cost of capital of these various assumptions is shown in Figure 12. Both approaches indicate that advantages exist in the use of some debt, with significant differences only occurring at higher levels of debt. However, many concerns will find it difficult to push their debt beyond 40% to 50% of total funds, or may simply not wish to because of the increased risk of significant loss or even bankruptcy. Hence, in practice, the use of extreme leverage seldom occurs and the two theories do not conflict at lower levels of debt.

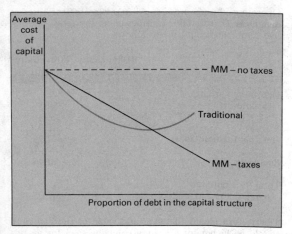

*Figure 12. Cost of capital – MM / traditional*

## DIVIDEND POLICY

The dividend decision is clearly related to the investment and financing decisions, and similar questions need to be asked.

**1.** Does dividend policy have any effect on the market price of a firm's equity?
**2.** If it does, what is the optimal dividend policy?

Following the logic of the earlier sections, it should be apparent, theoretically at least, that shareholders' wealth will be increased where new projects yield a return in excess of the cost of capital.

*In the absence of external funds* this means that dividend policy should **depend upon the investment opportunities** available to the firm. If the returns from new investments exceed the cost of funds, then profits should be retained so the new projects can be undertaken. If the returns are less, then the projects should be rejected and profits should be paid out as dividends. The point at which marginal returns from retentions equal the cost of equity should determine the level of dividends. This rule can be generalized to cover growth situations.

*If external funds are available* the arguments about capital structure also become important. The two schools of thought discussed in the last section can be extended to cover the dividend decision. The traditional arguments suggest that an optimal capital structure exists. Given that retentions are an extremely important source of equity capital, the dividend decision is clearly **likely to be influenced by the optimal capital structure** desired, as well as by the investment opportunities available and the cost of raising other funds. On the other hand, the MM view on capital structure suggests that valuation is independent of the capital structure. This argument can be extended to show that **valuation is also independent of dividend policy** given the following assumptions.

**1.** A perfect capital market.
**2.** Information is freely and immediately available.
**3.** No transactions costs.
**4.** No taxes.

These assumptions are not valid in the real world, and in practice there seems to be little doubt that the dividend decision is not as clear cut as might be implied from the above. Many reasons are given for the way in which profits are appropriated, but these vary from organization to organization and over time. Some reasons are fairly specific to individual organizations, but a number of **general trends and points** have been identified by empirical studies.

**1.** Corporations try to maintain a stable dividend.
**2.** Dividends are usually adjusted to follow trends in the corporation's earnings.
**3.** Dividend policies of large corporations differ from those of small and medium size firms.

**The relationship between earnings and dividends**
Dividends are paid some time after earnings have been made and generally follow much more smooth trends. This is attributable to a number of factors.

**1.** Directors are often reluctant to change the corporation's dividend in response to changes in circumstances that they believe are temporary.

**2.** Investors tend to look for actions which are consistent with past behavior. Sudden changes in behavior are open to misinterpretation.

**3.** Under conditions of uncertainty it may be considered sensible to delay payment of dividends until the pattern of future earnings becomes clearer.

## Dividends and size of organization
The empirical evidence in this area is somewhat conflicting, although the majority of research suggests that the proportion of earnings paid out as dividends tends to fall as size increases. On the other hand, it must be recognized that small organizations frequently experience difficulties in raising funds, and they may well be *forced* to reduce dividends in order to finance expansion, repay loans, etc.

## Other factors influencing dividend policy
Apart from the above factors, a number of other influences exist with regard to dividend policy.

**1. Government policy** The government has, at various times, attempted to control the level of dividends (e.g., the government froze the level of dividends when it instituted wage and price controls in the 70s).

**2. Legal restrictions.** Many states have laws that only allow companies to pay dividends from surplus capital. In addition some states do not allow companies to pay a dividend if it would make the firm insolvent.

**3. Stability of dividends** It may well be the case that share values *are* influenced by dividend policy. In particular, stable dividends may result in a lowering of the discount rate used by shareholders, either because such patterns of cash flow suit them better or because they associate less risk with such a policy. In either case, the stock's price is likely to be higher if the firm maintains a stable dividend.

**4. Stability of earnings** The more stable the earnings of an organization are, the more likely the organization will feel able to pay out a high proportion of its earnings. Less stable organizations will need to consider retaining more for contingencies.

**5. Liquidity** In order to pay out dividends there must be adequate profits *and* adequate liquid resources. Given that retained earnings are often automatically re-invested in plant and inventory, there is no necessary link between reserves and liquidity, and the liquidity constraint may be critical. This is typically the case with rapidly growing organizations, and in such cases the chances of high dividends are small. The need to repay existing debt may have a similar effect on dividends.

**6. Restrictions in debt contracts** Sometimes debt contracts include restrictions on the amount of dividends to be paid out. These must be complied with.

**7. Access to capital markets** Large, well-established organizations with records of profitability and some stability of earnings are likely to have relatively easy access to capital markets and other sources of external funds. Smaller, less well-established organizations will have far more restricted sources of funds and will probably need to rely on retentions to a much greater extent.

**8. Growth** The greater the growth rate, the higher retentions are likely to be.

**9. Return on investment** If an organization has very attractive investment opportunities available, i.e., better than those which are available to the shareholders as individuals, it will be wiser to retain funds to finance these investments rather than to pay them out as dividends.

**10. Control** Retained profits do not lead to any changes in the control of an organization whereas dividends followed by further fund raising might.

**11. The tax position of shareholders** If the directors of an organization are aware of the tax position of the majority of their shareholders, they may make dividend decisions which take this position into account. For example, a corporation closely held by a few taxpayers in high income tax brackets is likely to pay out low dividends and aim for increased stock price, since dividend income would be taxed at the same rate as regular income rather than the lower rate applied to capital gains. Also capital gains taxes are not paid until the stock is sold, which may be years in the future.

On the other hand, shareholders of other corporations may be more interested in a high dividend payout. Some balancing may need to take place, but there is evidence to suggest that the actual dividend payout policy has a considerable influence on the type of shareholder an organization attracts. This provides another argument in support of stability in a dividend policy.

### Conclusions on dividend policy
In the final analysis, management must balance the various factors referred to above. In practice, the dividend decision does seem to be a *positive* decision rather than a residual from investment decisions. Nevertheless, the last dividend paid seems to exert a strong influence on any future proposals, and increases usually occur only when management is sure that future dividends can be sustained at this new level.

## APPENDIX I

### Present value of $1

| Period | 2% | 5% | 8% | 10% | 12% | 16% | 20% |
|---|---|---|---|---|---|---|---|
| 1 | .980 | .952 | .926 | .909 | .893 | .862 | .833 |
| 2 | .961 | .907 | .857 | .826 | .797 | .743 | .694 |
| 3 | .942 | .864 | .794 | .751 | .712 | .641 | .579 |
| 4 | .924 | .823 | .735 | .683 | .636 | .552 | .482 |
| 5 | .906 | .784 | .681 | .621 | .567 | .476 | .402 |
| 6 | .888 | .746 | .630 | .564 | .507 | .410 | .335 |
| 7 | .871 | .711 | .583 | .513 | .452 | .354 | .279 |
| 8 | .853 | .677 | .540 | .467 | .404 | .305 | .233 |
| 9 | .837 | .645 | .500 | .424 | .361 | .263 | .194 |
| 10 | .820 | .614 | .463 | .386 | .322 | .227 | .162 |

## APPENDIX II

### Present value of an annuity of $1 each period.

| Period | 2% | 5% | 8% | 10% | 12% | 16% | 20% |
|---|---|---|---|---|---|---|---|
| 1 | 0.980 | 0.952 | 0.926 | 0.909 | 0.893 | 0.862 | 0.833 |
| 2 | 1.942 | 1.859 | 1.783 | 1.736 | 1.690 | 1.605 | 1.528 |
| 3 | 2.884 | 2.723 | 2.577 | 2.487 | 2.402 | 2.246 | 2.106 |
| 4 | 3.808 | 3.546 | 3.312 | 3.170 | 3.037 | 2.789 | 2.589 |
| 5 | 4.713 | 4.329 | 3.993 | 3.791 | 3.605 | 3.274 | 2.991 |
| 6 | 5.601 | 5.076 | 4.623 | 4.355 | 4.111 | 3.685 | 3.326 |
| 7 | 6.472 | 5.786 | 5.206 | 4.868 | 4.564 | 4.039 | 3.605 |
| 8 | 7.325 | 6.463 | 5.747 | 5.335 | 4.968 | 4.344 | 3.837 |
| 9 | 8.162 | 7.108 | 6.247 | 5.759 | 5.328 | 4.607 | 4.031 |
| 10 | 8.983 | 7.722 | 6.710 | 6.145 | 5.650 | 4.833 | 4.193 |

**APPENDIX III**

**Derivation of the optimum order quantity for stock**
Assume that inventory has been depleted to zero before a new delivery takes place and that:

$E$ = economic order quantity;
$C$ = the cost associated with placing each order;
$A$ = annual demand for (or usage of) the inventory item;
$H$ = the cost of holding one unit of inventory for one year.

Then the annual cost of holding a particular inventory item is the sum of two costs.

**1.** The cost of placing the orders $\left( \dfrac{A}{E} \times C \right)$

**2.** The cost of holding the inventory $\left( \dfrac{E}{2} \times H \right)$

These two costs give a total annual inventory holding of

$$\left( \frac{AC}{E} + \frac{EH}{2} \right)$$

This cost will be minimized when the above expression is differentiated with respect to $E$ and then equated to zero, i.e.,

$$0 = \left( \frac{-AC}{E^2} + \frac{H}{2} \right)$$

Therefore, $\dfrac{AC}{E^2} = \dfrac{H}{2}$ and $E^2 = \dfrac{2AC}{H}$

Therefore, $E = \sqrt{\dfrac{2AC}{H}}$

# Further Reading

Bierman, H. and Smidt, S., *The Capital Decision* (Collier-Macmillan, 1975)

Brealey, R. and Myers, S., *Principles of Corporate Finance* (McGraw-Hill, 1984)

Bromwich, M., *The Economics of Capital Budgeting* (Penguin, 1976)

*Federal Tax Course* (Prentice-Hall, 1980).

Franks, J. R. and Broyles, J. E., *Modern Managerial Finance* (John Wiley & Sons, 1979)

Freear, J., *The Management of Business Finance* (Pitman, 1980)

Levy, H. and Sarnat, M., *Capital Investment and Financial Decisions* (Prentice-Hall, 1982)

Lumby, S., *Investment Appraisal* (Nelson, 1981)

Merrett, A. J. and Sykes, A., *The Finance and Analysis of Capital Projects* (Longman, 1973)

Sharpe, William F., *Investments* (Prentice-Hall, 1981).

Stigum, M., *The Money Market: Myth, Reality, and Practice* (Dow Jones-Irwin, 1978).

Van Horne, J., *Financial Management and Policy* (Prentice-Hall, 1977).

Weston, J. F. and Brigham, E. F., *Managerial Finance* (Dryden Press, 1981).

# Glossary

**Accounting rate of return (ARR)** The net accounting profit from a particular project expressed as a percentage of the book value of the assets invested in that project.

**Annuity** A series of constant cash flows receivable for a specified number of years.

**Beta coefficient** A risk measure for assets held in portfolios. It is based on the degree of correlation between the expected returns from a particular asset and those from the market generally. Assets with high beta coefficients are the more risky and so would be expected to yield higher returns.

**Bonds** Interest bearing securities issued by both private and public sector organizations. Those of private sector organizations are also known as debentures.

**Business risk** That part of a business organization's risk which arises from its commercial activities. Business risk together with financial risk make up total risk.

**Capital budgeting** The evaluation of proposals for acquiring new fixed assets, so as to choose those projects which will provide the most benefit to the organization.

**Capital gains** The difference between the adjusted cost and the sales proceeds of capital (fixed) assets. These are taxed in the US and in most Western economies.

**Capital market** A market where organizations can raise capital by selling new securities. It is also a market for second-hand securities.

**Capital rationing** A situation in which not all positive NPV projects can be accepted because of a shortage of funds.

**Capital structure** The configuration of equity capital and loan capital in the long-term financing of an organization. It is sometimes referred to as the debt/equity relationship.

**Common shares.** Shares which entitle the holder to participate in all profits that remain after prior claims (e.g., preferred stockholders) have been met. They are usually the voting shares with which control is exerted.

**Corporation tax** A levy on the trading profits and capital gains of US corporations.

**Correlation** The extent to which variations in the value of one variable are associated with variations in that of another variable. For example, it is generally true that the returns from any particular asset are correlated with returns from the economy generally.

**Cost of capital** The price in terms of dividends, interest rates, etc., that an organization must pay for the capital it uses. It is also the discount rate which should be applied to investment projects when assessing them under the net present value criterion.

**Coupon rate** The rate of interest paid on the nominal (or par) value of fixed return securities. Unless the securities have a market value equal to their nominal value the actual yield will not be equal to the coupon rate.

**Cumulative preferred shares** These are preferred shares on which a failure to pay the full dividend in any year gives the holders the right to insist on both the arrears of dividend and the current dividend being paid in a future year before a dividend on the ordinary shares is paid.

**Current ratio** The ratio of current assets to current liabilities, used in assessing adequacy of working capital and liquidity of an organization.

**Debenture** A loan (usually long term) evidenced by a deed.

**Debt/equity ratio** The relationship between debt and equity.

**Decision trees** Graphical devices for assessing the relationship between decisions to be taken and possible occurrences. Frequently, probabilities are associated with each "branch".

**Depreciation** Accounting reduction in the book value of an asset may be charged against income for tax purposes.

**Discounted cash flow techniques** The use of discounting techniques to ensure comparability of cash flows occurring at different times.

**Discounting** Reducing future cash flows to their "present value" to take account of the time value of money. The amount by which a particular cash flow would be reduced depends on the discount rate used and the length of time before the cash flow will occur.

**Dividend yield** The return which arises as a cash dividend, expressed as a percentage of the market price of a share.

**Dividends** Distributions of profits, usually in cash, made by companies to their shareholders. The amount of dividend each shareholder receives depends on the rate of dividend per share and the number of shares held.

**Efficient market** One in which all information about the commodity dealt in is speedily and rationally reflected in prices.

**Equity** The risk-bearing portion of the long-term capital of a business organization. For a company it is the share capital and reserves.

**Factoring** An arrangement where a business organization raises finance against its trade debtors. Usually the factor pays the organization an agreed proportion of the face value of sales invoices. The factor may also provide an insurance service for bad debts and an administrative service for debt collection.

**Financial assets** Securities in various organizations, thus representing only an indirect investment in real assets.

**Financial risk** That part of a business organization's risk which arises from being partly financed by loan capital. Financial risk together with business risk make up total risk.

**Flow of funds statement** An accounting statement which sets out the sources and applications of the liquid assets of an organization for a period of time.

**Gearing** see Leverage.

**Interest rate risk** The risk borne by a lender that interest rates in the economy will rise, causing a fall in the capital value of the loan.

**Internal rate of return (IRR)** The discount rate for a project which will give a zero net present value. It is the rate of return or yield that a particular project will give.

**Investment banks** Banks which act as advisors to

organizations in respect of raising capital and which assist in the provision of development capital through loans and/or equity, usually with a view to that organization obtaining a quotation at some time in the future.

**Investment Tax Credit (ITC)** Amounts which organizations may deduct from profits to arrive at their taxable profit, as an allowance for the cost of certain fixed assets.

**Issue costs** The costs involved with making an issue of new securities. They include the legal and accounting fees as well as stationery and general administrative costs.

**Leasing** An arrangement where one party, the lessor, owns an asset which it allows the other party, the lessee, to use in consideration of regular rental payments.

**Leverage** A situation which exists when only part of the long-term finance of an organization is supplied by the ordinary shareholders, the remainder being supplied by preference shareholders, loan creditors and others who are entitled to a fixed return on their investment. Leverage is also known as gearing.

**Liquid assets** Those assets which are in the form of cash or which may quickly be turned into cash.

**Liquid ratio** The ratio of liquid assets to current liabilities, used to assess the adequacy of liquid funds of an organization.

**Liquidation** The act of bringing the life of a company to an end. It may be initiated by either the shareholders or the creditors, depending on the circumstances.

**Listed company** A company which has satisfied the council of the Stock Exchange in its requirements, a necessary prerequisite before Stock Exchange members are allowed to deal in the shares. It is also known as a listed company and is a company whose shares can be traded on the Stock Exchange.

**Marginal cost of funds** The rate that will have to be paid to raise the next dollar of funds. This cost will depend on the current financial position of the organization and on the purpose to which the new funds are to be put.

**Mortgage** A loan which is secured against a particular asset, usually land and/or buildings.

**Net present value (NPV)** The sum of the discounted cash flows of an investment project. Theoretically, it is the net increase (if positive) or decrease (if negative) in the wealth of the investor if he undertakes the project.

**Nominal value** The par value of a security. This is the book value of the security as shown in the organization's balance sheet. It is also the value on which interest and dividends are calculated when they are expressed as percentages.

**Opportunity costs** The returns available on the next best alternative; the loss of funds arising from taking one particular course of action instead of this next best alternative.

**Optimal capital structure** The configuration of equity and debt which gives rise to the lowest weighted average cost of capital, and therefore the highest total value for an organization.

**Overheads** Costs incurred to facilitate the activity of the business as a whole, which cannot be specifically identified with one particular product.

**Payback period** The length of time before an investment outlay will be covered by the net cash upflows arising from it.

**Perpetual bond** An interest-bearing security which is not redeemable and will, in theory, continue to pay interest for ever.

**Personal deductions** Deductions that an individual taxpayer may make from his total income to arrive at the taxable income.

**Portfolio effect** The reduction of specific risk which can be effected by holding a number of different and ideally unrelated risky assets as opposed to just one risky asset.

**Preferred stock** Shares which entitle the owner to receive the first slice of any dividend paid by the company. The size of the dividend is usually determined by a stated percentage.

**Price–earnings ratio** The relationship between the market price of a share and earnings per share.

**Prospectus** A document which the law compels companies to issue when they wish to raise new equity capital from the public. It contains various items of information about the company and its recent trading record.

**Redeemable securities** Stocks and bonds which the issuing organization may call in or repay, compensating the security holders with an amount of money which is usually predetermined. Sometimes redemption is made at a premium.

**Replacement cost** The price that would have to be paid to replace an asset with another of similar condition and usefulness.

**Required rate of return** Return required by investors if they are to invest in a particular security or project.

**Retained Earnings** Company profits or gains which are retained within the business, as opposed to being distributed to shareholders as dividends. They represent, along with share capital, the owners' investment in the company.

**Rights issue** An issue of stock, usually at a price below the current market price of the stock, offered to existing stockholders. The stockholders may choose to sell their "rights" to buy these shares to a third party.

**Risk** A situation where the precise outcome of an action is unknown but the possible outcomes and their individual likelihood of occurrence is known.

**Risk premium** An "extra" return required by investors to justify investing in risky securities.

**Salvage value** The proceeds which would be expected from selling an asset, after deduction of any costs of disposal.

**Secured loan** A loan where the principal, and possibly interest as well, is secured on some asset of the borrowing organization such that if the borrower defaults the lender may seize the asset and sell it to repay the amount owed.

**Security** A revenue earning investment which can be traded (e.g., on a stock exchange). These include ordinary shares, preferred shares and debentures.

**Sensitivity analysis** A technique for assessing which

factors concerned with a decision are the most critical. The effect of changes in relevant variables on the overall results of the project are calculated. From this it should be possible to determine the nature of the problems to be faced, and also to form some opinion as to the riskiness of the project.

**Share** A specific proportion of the equity or owners' investment in a corporation.

**Simulation** A "pretend" run of a planned course of action, with possible events being introduced (usually randomly) in an attempt to estimate how successful the action is likely to be. Probabilities are often used.

**Specialist** A member of the stock exchange who acts as a "stall holder" on the floor of the Stock Exchange in respect of specific securities in which he specializes. Stock jobbers may not deal directly with the public but only with stockbrokers and other floor traders.

**Specific risk** That part of the total risk which is specific to a particular organization or industry. It can be virtually eliminated by holding a relatively small portfolio of investments in different industries. It is also referred to as unsystematic risk.

**Stock dividend** Reserves of companies which are converted into shares to be distributed to shareholders, at no cost, in proportion to their existing holdings.

**Stock Exchange** A market where securities may be bought and sold. Most securities traded are second-hand, but often new issues of securities are sold through a stock exchange.

**Stock Exchange listing** Approval by a stock exchange of the credibility of an organization results in the securities being placed on a list of those which the exchange will allow its members to trade in. Thus, the listing means that the securities may be traded on the stock exchange. Also known as a "Stock Exchange Quotation".

**Stockbroker** A member of a stock exchange who acts as an agent for his clients in the buying and selling of securities on the floor of the exchange. He typically carries out other functions, including giving investment advice to his clients.

**Synergy** The phenomenon of the whole being greater than the sum of the parts. The word is often applied to business mergers. In this context it means that the total earnings of the merged operation will be greater than the sum of the current earnings of the parties to the merger.

**Systematic risk** That part of the total risk which arises from macroeconomic factors such as general trade recessions. It is also referred to as non-specific risk.

**Take over** The act of one organization acquiring the business of another. This is usually achieved by the acquiring organization buying sufficient shares in the target organization to give it effective control.

**Target** A term often ascribed to an organization which another organization is seeking to take over. Targets are sometimes referred to as "victims".

**Tax credit** When a taxpayer receives some income from which tax has already been deducted, he is said to have a tax credit. This is set against his tax liability for that year.

**Taxable income** The income on which a taxpayer will be assessed for tax.

**Trade credit** The provision of goods and services on an interest free short-term credit basis, i.e., payment is not required until after a specified period.

**Underwriting** A process of "guaranteeing" new issues of securities by promising to acquire any which remain unsold by a certain date.

**Unlisted securities market** This comprises those securities dealt in by members of the stock exchange which have not been subject to the rigorous investigation associated with a full stock exchange listing. Most of these securities are those of smaller organizations for whom the costs of obtaining a full listing would not be justified.

**Utility function** The relationship between monetary values and associated satisfactions.

**Valuation model** An equation or device for placing values on assets, particularly applied to securities.

**Weighted average cost of capital** The average of the costs of the various sources of funds weighted according to the amount of funds (by market value) from each source.

**Working capital** That part of an organization's assets which, in the normal course of trading, are translated into other assets. Typically, working capital consists of stock-in-trade, plus short-term debtors, plus cash, less short-term creditors.

**Yield** *see* Internal rate of return.